Muscle Mechanics

SECOND EDITION

Everett Aaberg

HUMAN KINETICS

Library of Congress Cataloging-in-Publication Data

Aaberg, Everett, 1963-
  Muscle mechanics / Everett Aaberg.-- 2nd ed.
    p. cm.
  Includes bibliographical references and index.
  ISBN 0-7360-6695-0 (soft cover)
  1. Weight training. 2. Exercise. I. Title.
  GV546.A23 2006
  613.7'13--dc22

                    2005020256

ISBN-10: 0-7360-6695-0
ISBN-13: 978-0-7360-6695-2

Acquisitions Editor: Martin Barnard
Developmental Editor: Leigh Keylock
Assistant Editor: Carla Zych
Copyeditor: Patrick Connolly
Proofreader: Julie Marx Goodreau
Indexer: Bobbi Swanson
Graphic Designer: Robert Reuther
Graphic Artist: Francine Hamerski
Photo Manager: Dan Wendt
Cover Designer: American Fitness Professionals & Associates
Photographer (interior): Sarah Ritz
Art Manager: Kareema McLendon-Foster
Illustrators: Figure 9.1 by Kareema McLendon-Foster; muscle drawings on pages 50-186 by Hoc K. Kho, Brian F. Wilson, Shannon Bean, and Meredith A. Phillips/Nucleus Medical Art, Inc.; all other illustrations by Scott Beckley
Printer: Custom Color Graphics

Human Kinetics books are available at special discounts for bulk purchase. Special editions or book excerpts can also be created to specification. For details, contact the Special Sales Manager at Human Kinetics.

Printed in the United States of America   10 9 8 7 6 5 4 3

Human Kinetics
Web site: www.HumanKinetics.com

United States: Human Kinetics
P.O. Box 5076
Champaign, IL 61825-5076
800-747-4457
e-mail: humank@hkusa.com

Canada: Human Kinetics
475 Devonshire Road, Unit 100
Windsor, ON N8Y 2L5
800-465-7301 (in Canada only)
e-mail: info@hkcanada.com

Europe: Human Kinetics
107 Bradford Road
Stanningley
Leeds LS28 6AT, United Kingdom
+44 (0)113 255 5665
e-mail: hk@hkeurope.com

Australia: Human Kinetics
57A Price Avenue
Lower Mitcham, South Australia 5062
08 8372 0999
e-mail: info@hkaustralia.com

New Zealand: Human Kinetics
Division of Sports Distributors NZ Ltd.
P.O. Box 300 226 Albany
North Shore City, Auckland
0064 9 448 1207
e-mail: info@humankinetics.co.nz

Muscle Mechanics

SECOND EDITION

Contents

Preface

Over the last two decades, resistance training has drastically risen in popularity and demand. Health clubs, racquet clubs, country clubs, hotels, apartment complexes, hospitals, and even corporate wellness centers have been gradually dedicating more space, buying more equipment, and devoting more attention to providing resistance training for their patrons and employees. A remarkable amount of research that documents the numerous health benefits associated with resistance training has been amassed. Information on these benefits has emerged in professional textbooks as well as commercial and consumer books and overflowed into magazines of all kinds. The mounting facts regarding resistance training's potential to improve health and human performance, along with its ability to sculpt the human physique more than any other modality of exercise, ensure that this trend will continue to grow in the coming years.

However, if you want to accomplish any goal with resistance training—whether the aim is rehabilitation, optimal athletic performance, bodybuilding, fat loss, or simply overall health—efficient exercise selection and optimal technique are critical for success. This fact is confirmed by most fitness professionals, yet there are still very few books available that present sound scientific rationale for the exercise selections and techniques that they present. As a result, people who are actively attempting to gain improvements from resistance training are left with little direction for selecting the best exercises to accomplish their goals, and even less information on what exactly constitutes efficient and safe exercise technique.

Deciding what criteria should be used in determining "efficient" or "safe" technique for resistance training is often a topic for debate and seems to be extremely subject to opinion. However, an enormous amount of scientific data exists on which to base many elements of resistance training technique. Through in-depth study of anatomical design and specific joint structure, we can deduce much in regard to the body's intended functional abilities and also its natural limitations. This information combined with the application of basic physics and biomechanics can assist in developing definite guidelines for selecting and performing resistance training exercises for more efficiency and reduced risk.

The primary purpose of *Muscle Mechanics* is to teach efficient and safe exercise technique and to provide you with the scientific information necessary for better selecting resistance exercises and designing resistance training programs in order to achieve all of your performance and aesthetic goals.

Muscle Mechanics presents many contemporary resistance training exercises aimed at improving biomechanical function and movement performance but also includes several traditional exercises that are time proven for their effectiveness in developing the physique. However, all the resistance training exercises (both traditional and contemporary) have been analyzed and modified, through application of the scienctific principles and infusion of the specialized techniques presented in this book. Previous versions of this book have served as instructional texts in several colleges and universities and as an instruction manual for many fitness organizations around the world such as the renowned Cooper Institute. Thousands of professional trainers have taught and successfully used many of the exercises and associated techniques presented in this text to better develop the abilities and aesthetics of their clients and themselves. Learn and apply the information herein. Integrate the exercises and use the techniques with confidence, but always check with your doctor before beginning any exercise program.

Anatomical Design and Function

Muscle Mechanics focuses on providing instruction on a collection of the safest and most efficient resistance training exercises possible based on the structure and function of the human body. Therefore, before learning any specific exercises and techniques for improving the performance or the aesthetics of the body, you should first gain a general understanding of how the body is constructed and designed to move. The human body is an extremely sophisticated machine with a very large number of components that combine to produce an infinite variety of postures and movements. These components are highly integrated and function together as interdependent systems and subsystems.

A contemporary view of functional anatomy often presented by authors and experts describes the body as being composed of three basic interdependent systems. These three systems are referred to as the *control system* (or sensorimotor system), the *active system* (or muscular system), and the *passive system* (or skeletal system). All three systems must work together synergistically to produce any motion or even to just stabilize the body in the presence of outside forces such as gravity. Therefore, since all exercise requires unique combinations of both movement and stabilization, any exercise will impress a training effect on all three systems, not just the targeted muscles. This makes technique more critical than many people realize. Every exercise performed will not only affect the body's "hardware," which consists of the joints and muscles of the active and passive systems, but will also imprint information on the "software," which consists of the programmable features of the control system.

To perform any body movement, whether voluntarily or through reflex actions, the control system issues commands to the active system to initiate the unique concert of muscle actions necessary for stabilizing and moving the passive system. These three systems are truly interdependent such that even automated actions such as breathing, coughing, sneezing, or flinching in response to pain all require specific integrated and coordinated actions. The following sections cover the movement responsibilities of each system, beginning with the passive-skeletal system, then the active-muscular system, and then the control-sensorimotor system. Figure 1.1 shows a schematic representation of these three systems and their interdependent relationships.

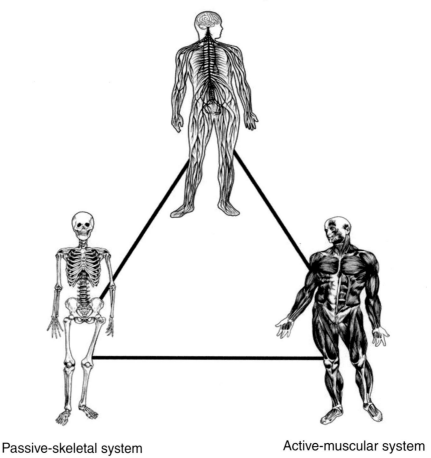

Control-sensorimotor system

Passive-skeletal system

Active-muscular system

Figure 1.1 The three systems of human movement.

The Passive System

The passive system is composed of the skeleton, joints, and associated connective tissues. It is termed "passive" because there is no force directly produced by this system. It is a reactive system that can only transfer forces produced by the active system as commanded by the control system. The passive system provides the structures and levers that give us the ability to utilize internal forces to move the body and interact with the environment.

The Skeleton

At birth, the human body contains approximately 270 bones, some of which are designed to fuse as the body grows. By the time a person becomes an adult, the skeleton normally consists of only 206 bones, which provide a lightweight yet protective and supportive structure that ultimately provides for all movement of the body. Figure 1.2 details the construction of the human skeleton for easy reference. The skeleton performs three main mechanical functions:

1. It protects certain organs such as the brain, spinal cord, heart, and lungs.
2. It acts as a supportive framework for the body.
3. It acts as a system of levers that the muscles can act on to stabilize and move the body.

1. Cranium
2. Clavicle
3. Sternum
4. Rib
5. Humerus
6. Radius
7. Ulna
8. Pubis
9. Carpus
10. Metacarpals
11. Phalanges
12. Femur
13. Patella
14. Tibia
15. Fibula
16. Tarsus
17. Metatarsals
18. Phalanges
19. Cervical vertebrae (7)
20. Scapula
21. Thoracic vertebrae (12)
22. Lumbar vertebrae (5)
23. Illium
24. Sacrum
25. Ishium

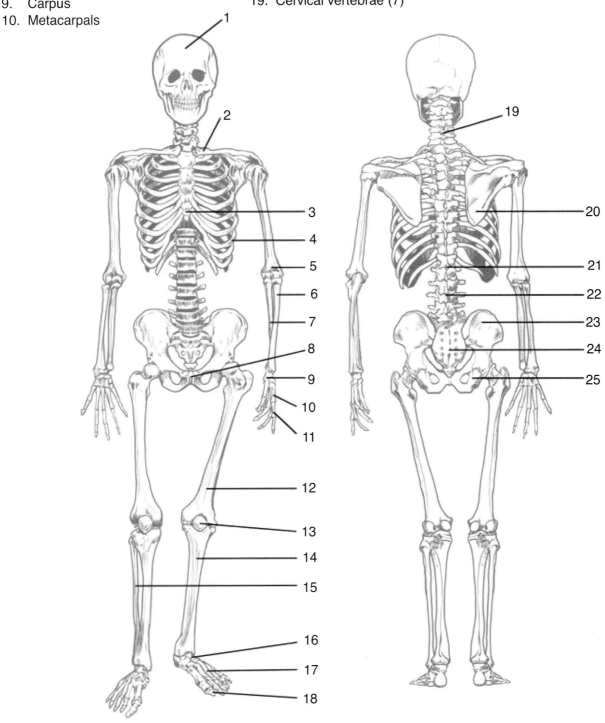

Figure 1.2 The passive-skeletal system.

The bones of the skeleton are typically divided into two main groups, the axial skeleton and the appendicular skeleton. The adult *axial skeleton* is composed of approximately 80 bones that form the skull, spine, and rib cage. It provides the foundation for the body and protects the brain, spinal cord, and major organs. The *appendicular skeleton* is composed of 126 bones that make up the scapula and the upper limbs as well as the pelvis and the lower limbs. This collection of bones provides the primary lever systems that enable a person to move the body and any external objects.

The Joints

Joints are, simply stated, the meeting place of two or more bones. The bone endings, the associated connective tissues that hold them together, and the sensory receptors in and around the joint are all vital components of the passive-skeletal system. Joints are uniquely designed to allow for certain amounts and directions of movement while also providing certain levels of stability. There are three structural classifications of joints, each with distinct levels of possible articulation, or available movement: fibrous, cartilaginous, and synovial joints.

Fibrous joints allow for very little, if any, movement because of the small amount of space between bone endings. They include the joints of the skull, the joints between the radius and ulna of the lower arm, and the distal connection of the fibula and tibia of the lower leg.

Cartilaginous joints allow for some movement, but their capacity for movement is limited because of the proportionally higher collagen to elastin fiber compositions of these joints. Examples of cartilaginous joints are those that connect the ribs to the sternum.

Synovial joints account for most of the joints of the human body, and they are individually designed with considerable variance in their range of motion. The three types of synovial joints are categorized by the number of directions in which they can rotate around a given axis: uniaxial, biaxial, and multiaxial joints (see figure 1.3, a-c).

Uniaxial joints have only one direction of rotation and operate much like a hinge. The elbow and the phalangeal joints of the fingers are examples of uniaxial joints. *Biaxial joints,* such as the wrist, ankle, and knee (when flexed), allow for movement in two perpendicular planes. *Multi-*

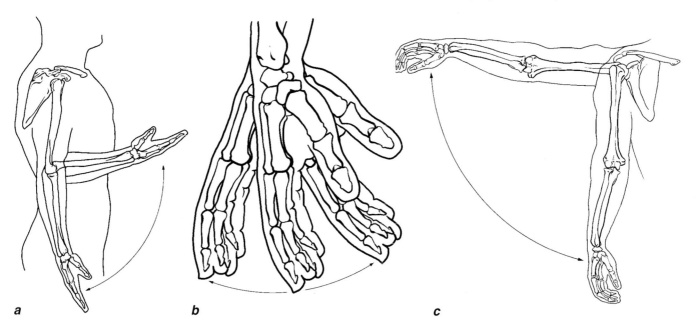

a   b   c

Figure 1.3 Examples of the three types of synovial joints: *(a)* uniaxial, *(b)* biaxial, and *(c)* multiaxial.

axial joints, such as the shoulder and hip, allow for movement in all three planes of motion and therefore provide us with the greatest degrees and varieties of possible movement.

Passive Connective Tissue

A joint's capacity for movement is only in part determined by the structure and congruence of the bones themselves. Connective tissues hold the bones together and regulate the type, direction, and range of motion between the bone endings. Two types of passive connective tissues that assist with stabilization and regulation of joint movement are ligaments and joint capsules.

Ligaments connect bone to bone and consist primarily of strong collagen fibers arranged parallel to each other with only small amounts of elastic fiber. They are designed to restrict joint movement within specific directions and within specific ranges of movement. Ligaments are not capable of any significant stretching without deformation or tearing. Therefore, they are at risk when movement is forced at a joint in directions or at ranges outside their genetically determined limits. Ligaments can be separate or can be part of the joint capsule, and they can be located outside or inside the capsule itself. Ligament placement and design are relative to the designed function of the joint and its combined needs for mobility and stability.

Joint capsules enclose the joint, creating a cavity that holds fluid in the joint and also assists in the transfer of forces from bone to bone. The capsule is typically composed of two or more layers of regular collagenous tissue that form a sleeve around the joint. The parallel collagen fiber arrangements of each layer are typically laid down at different angles to the adjacent layers. This enables the capsule to allow for movement in certain directions and still strongly resist movement in other directions. Capsules assist with joint stability and can tear or become deformed when overstretched.

Cartilage is another substance found at synovial joints. It does not play a connective role but should also be considered when analyzing joint movement and joint forces. Cartilage can also be damaged as a result of excessive joint movement or through exposure to high or frequent compressive, distractive, or shearing forces. Cartilage damage is often permanent and can occur suddenly or gradually depending on the range, force, or repetition of joint motion.

Hyaline or *articular cartilage* is a smooth, slick protective covering over bone endings at synovial joints that assists with ease of joint movement. Articular cartilage is well constructed to absorb certain levels of force and friction, but excessive pressure, repetitive mechanical wear, or movement exceeding the designed limits of the joint can all contribute to degeneration of articular cartilage, which can lead to osteoarthritis. Once osteoarthritis begins in a joint, it typically continues to deteriorate joint surfaces, causing inflammation, pain, and decreased joint function.

Fibrocartilage contains high concentrations of collagenous fibers and is specially designed for absorbing shock. It is a thick, rubberlike material found in the vertebral discs of the spine, the menisci of the knee, the pubis symphysis of the pelvis, and at other joints in need of the extra cartilage support or padding between bone surfaces. Though resilient, fibrocartilage is also susceptible to thinning, tearing, folding, and rupturing under high levels of, or frequent exposure to, impact forces and friction. The body's natural replacement of fibrocartilage is limited, which can often leave the joint with little or no disc substance and painful, inefficient joint movement.

Isolated Joint Mechanics

Any movement of a joint requires interaction of all three systems and is not just a result of the muscles pulling on bones. The human body is also capable of producing an infinite number of joint movements that do not occur in any singular plane. However, for the purpose of

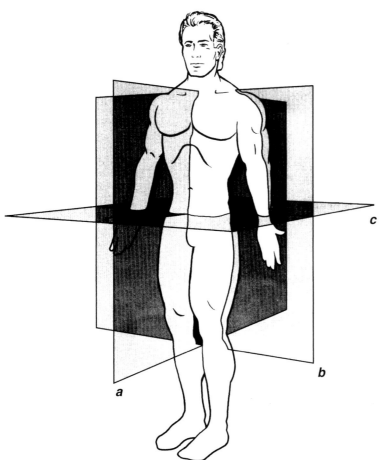

establishing a better understanding of basic muscle mechanics, joint motion will be presented in a traditional "three-plane format" (median, frontal, and horizontal) as pictured in figure 1.4, and the information will incorporate the following premises:

- The joint movement is beginning from a preset anatomical standing position.
- Each joint movement is considered in isolation and is performed in only one general plane of motion.
- Only the muscles directly involved with the specific movement of that joint are recognized.

Figure 1.4 The planes of motion: *(a)* the median plane, *(b)* the frontal plane, and *(c)* the horizontal plane.

Joint Motions of the Median Plane

The median plane, also known as the sagittal plane, divides the body down the middle into left and right halves. Most human movement takes place predominantly in the median plane. The joint motions of flexion and extension are the primary movements of the median plane and occur at the ankle, knee, hip, spine, shoulder, elbow, wrist, and neck. Scapular protraction and retraction are also considered median plane movements.

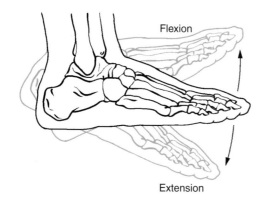

Ankle Flexion (Dorsiflexion)

Tibialis anterior
Extensor hallucis longus
Extensor digitorum longus
Peroneus tertius

Ankle Extension (Plantar Flexion)

Peroneus longus
Peroneus brevis
Triceps surae
Flexor hallucis longus
Tibialis posterior
Flexor digitorum longus

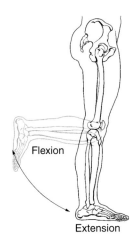

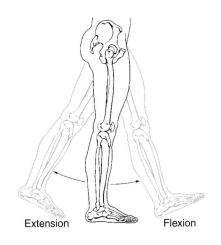

Knee Flexion

Biceps femoris (long and short heads)

Semitendinosus

Semimembranosus

Popliteus

Gastrocnemius

Sartorius

Gracilis

Knee Extension

Vastus lateralis

Vastus medialis

Vastus intermedius

Rectus femoris

Tensor fasciae latae

Gluteus maximus (superficial portion)

Hip Flexion

Psoas

Iliacus

Rectus femoris

Tensor fasciae latae

Gluteus minimus and medius (anterior portions)

Sartorius

Pectineus

Gracilis

Hip Extension

Gluteus maximus

Biceps femoris (long head)

Semimembranosus

Semitendinosus

Gluteus medius (posterior portion)

Adductor magnus

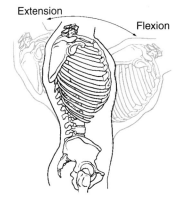

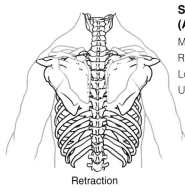

Scapular Retraction (Adduction)

Mid trapezius

Rhomboids

Lower trapezius

Upper trapezius

Trunk Flexion

Rectus abdominis

External obliques (bilateral contraction)

Internal obliques (bilateral contraction)

Trunk Extension

Spinalis group

Longissimus group

Iliocostalis group

Transversospinalis group

Interspinalis

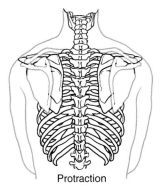

Scapular Protraction (Abduction)

Mid serratus anterior

Upper serratus anterior (superior)

Lower serratus anterior (inferior)

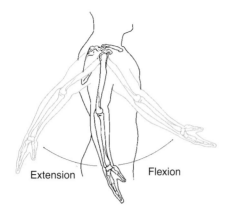

Shoulder Flexion

Anterior deltoid
Pectoralis major
Coracobrachialis

Shoulder Extension

Latissimus dorsi
Posterior deltoid
Teres minor

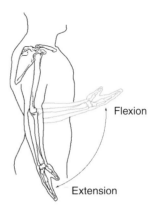

Elbow Flexion

Biceps brachii
Brachioradialis
Brachialis

Elbow Extension

Triceps long head
Triceps lateral head
Triceps medial head (deep head)
Anconeus .

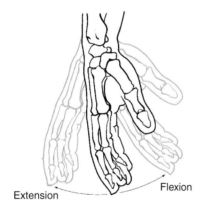

Wrist Flexion

Flexor carpi radialis
Palmaris longus
Flexor carpi ulnaris

Wrist Extension

Extensor carpi radialis longus
Extensor carpi radialis brevis
Extensor carpi ulnaris

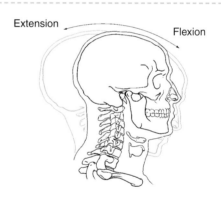

Neck Flexion

Longus colli (bilateral contraction)
Rectus capitis (bilateral contraction)
Longus capitis (bilateral contraction)
Sternocleidomastoid (bilateral contraction)
Suprahyoid group (accessory)
Infrahyoid group (accessory)

Neck Extension

Splenius capitis (bilateral contraction)
Splenius cervicis (bilateral contraction)
Spinalis capitis (bilateral contraction)*
Semispinalis capitis (bilateral contraction)*
Spinalis thoracis
Levator scapulae (bilateral contraction)
Trapezius (bilateral contraction)
   *When spine is fixed or stabilized

Joint Motions of the Frontal Plane

The frontal plane, sometimes presented as the coronal plane, divides the body through the side into front and back halves. Joint movements of the frontal plane include abduction and adduction of the wrist, shoulder, and hip; inversion and eversion of the ankle; scapular elevation, depression, upward rotation, and downward rotation; and lateral flexion of the spine and neck.

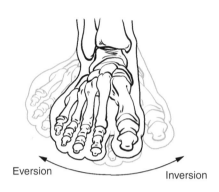

Eversion   Inversion

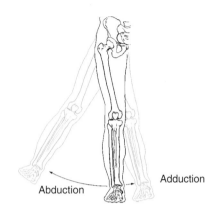

Abduction   Adduction

Ankle Inversion (Partial Supination)

Extensor hallucis longus
Tibialis anterior
Tibialis posterior
Flexor digitorum longus
Flexor hallucis longus
Triceps surae

Ankle Eversion (Partial Pronation)

Peroneus longus
Peroneus brevis
Peroneus tertius
Extensor digitorum longus (lateral portion)

Hip Adduction

Adductor magnus
Adductor longus
Adductor brevis
Pectineus
Gracilis
Psoas
Iliacus

Hip Abduction

Gluteus medius
Gluteus minimus
Tensor fasciae latae
Gluteus maximus (superficial portion)
Piriformis
Obturators
Gemelli
Sartorius

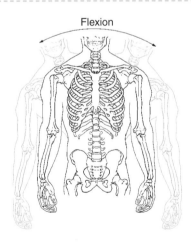

Flexion

Trunk Lateral Flexion

Internal obliques (unilateral contraction)
Quadratus lumborum (unilateral contraction)
Rectus abdominis (unilateral contraction)
Erector spinae groups (unilateral contraction)
Latissimus dorsi (unilateral contraction)
Transversospinalis group (unilateral contraction)
Intertransversarii (unilateral contraction)

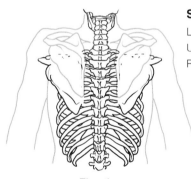

Elevation

Scapular Elevation

Levator scapulae
Upper trapezius
Rhomboids

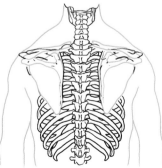

Depression

Scapular Depression

Lower trapezius
Lower serratus anterior
Pectoralis minor
Subclavius (via the clavicle)

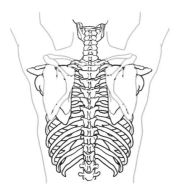

Scapular Upward Rotation

Upper trapezius

Lower trapezius

Upper serratus anterior (superior)

Upward rotation

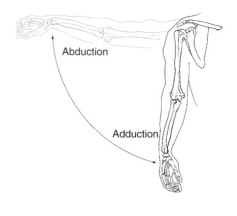

Abduction

Adduction

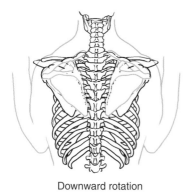

Downward rotation

Scapular Downward Rotation

Rhomboids

Levator scapulae

Shoulder Adduction (Frontal Extension)

Latissimus dorsi

Pectoralis major

Teres major

Teres minor (accessory)

Shoulder Abduction (Frontal Flexion)

Deltoids

Supraspinatus

Infraspinatus (accessory)

Long head biceps (accessory)

Upper subscapularis (accessory)

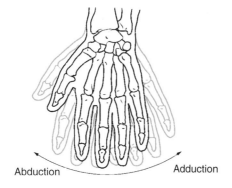

Abduction

Adduction

Wrist Adduction

Flexor carpi ulnaris

Extensor carpi ulnaris

Wrist Abduction

Flexor carpi radialis

Extensor carpi radialis longus

Extensor carpi radialis brevis

Lateral flexion

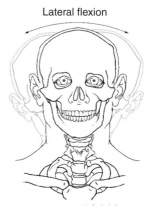

Neck Lateral Flexion

Scalenus group (unilateral contraction)

Sternocleidomastoid (unilateral contraction)

Longus colli (unilateral contraction)

Rectus capitis (unilateral contraction)

Longus capitis (unilateral contraction)

Splenius capitis (unilateral contraction)

Splenius cervicis (unilateral contraction)

Spinalis capitis (unilateral contraction)

Semispinalis capitis (unilateral contraction)

Trapezius (unilateral contraction)

Joint Motions of the Horizontal Plane

The horizontal plane, also referred to as the transverse plane, cuts the body horizontally into lower and upper halves. Movements of the horizontal plane include internal and external rotation of the knee, hip, and shoulder; horizontal flexion and extension of the shoulder; inversion and eversion of the ankle;* supination and pronation of the radioulnar joint; and spinal and neck rotation.

*Supination and pronation of the ankle are special-case movements (not pictured) and require combining ankle extension with inversion and combining ankle flexion with eversion respectively.

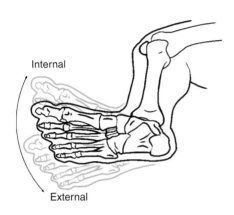

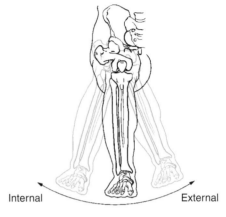

Knee Internal Rotation (Medial Rotation)

Sartorius
Semitendinosus
Semimembranosus
Gracilis
Popliteus

Knee External Rotation (Lateral Rotation)

Tensor fasciae latae
Gluteus maximus (superficial portion)
Biceps femoris long head
Biceps femoris short head

Hip Internal Rotation (Medial Rotation)

Gluteus medius
Gluteus minimus
Tensor fasciae latae

Hip External Rotation (Lateral Rotation)

Gluteus maximus
Gluteus minimus
Piriformis
Obturators
Gemelli
Quadratus femoris
Biceps femoris (long head)

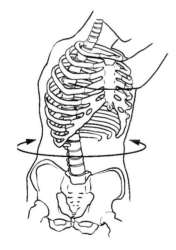

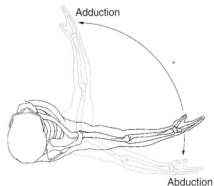

Trunk Rotation

Erector spinae groups (unilateral contraction)
Transversospinalis group (unilateral contraction)
External obliques (unilateral contraction)
Internal obliques (contralateral contraction)

Shoulder Horizontal Adduction (Horizontal Flexion)

Pectoralis major (sternal)
Pectoralis major (clavicular)
Anterior deltoid
Subclavius
Coracobrachialis (accessory)
Biceps brachii (accessory)
Scapular protractors

Shoulder Horizontal Abduction (Horizontal Extension)

Posterior deltoid
Infraspinatus
Teres minor
Scapular retractors (accessory)

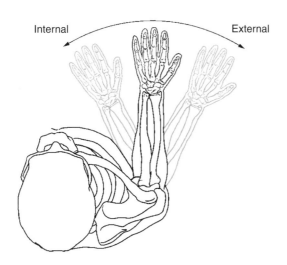

Internal   External

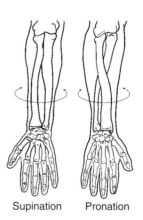

Supination   Pronation

Shoulder Internal Rotation (Medial Rotation)

Subscapularis
Latissimus dorsi
Pectoralis major
Teres major
Anterior deltoid

Shoulder External Rotation (Lateral Rotation)

Infraspinatus
Teres minor
Posterior deltoid

Radioulnar Pronation

Pronator teres
Pronator quadratus
Brachioradialis

Radioulnar Supination

Biceps brachii
Supinator

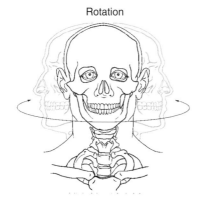

Rotation

Neck Rotation

Sternocleidomastoid (unilateral contraction)*
Trapezius (unilateral contraction)*
Longus colli (unilateral contraction)
Rectus capitis (unilateral contraction)
Splenius capitis (unilateral contraction)
Splenius cervicis (unilateral contraction)
Spinalis capitis (unilateral contraction)
Semispinalis capitis (unilateral contraction)
    *Contralateral rotation

The Active System

The active system is composed of the muscles and their associated tendons and fascia. Any joint movement requires more muscle action than just those directly responsible for the actual limb or body movement. Numerous other muscles are working simultaneously in order to maintain the person's center of gravity, stabilize the spine, control other joints, or neutralize undesired effects of the motion. In fact, more than 600 voluntary muscles may be playing various roles in an integrated manner in order to optimally perform any desired movement. Figure 1.5 depicts the human muscular system with most of the major voluntary muscles identified.

1. Platysma
2. Deltoid
3. Pectoralis major
4. Biceps brachii
5. Pronator teres
6. Flexor group
7. External oblique
8. Rectus abdominis
9. Adductors
10. Sartorius
11. Rectus femoris
12. Vastus medialis
13. Peroneus longus
14. Tibialis anterior
15. Coracobrachialis
16. Brachialis
17. Internal oblique
18. Brachioradialis
19. Flexor digitorum superficialis

20. Trapezius
21. Deltoid
22. Triceps brachii
23. Latissimus dorsi
24. Extensor group
25. Gluteus maximus
26. Iliotibial tract
27. Biceps femoris
28. Semitendinosus

29. Gastrocnemius
30. Splenius capitis
31. Levator scapula
32. Rhomboids
33. Infraspinatus
34. Teres minor
35. Teres major
36. Erector spinae
37. Serratus posterior inferior
38. Gluteus minimus
39. Gluteus medius (cut)
40. Piriformis
41. Semimembranosus
42. Plantaris
43. Popliteus
44. Soleus

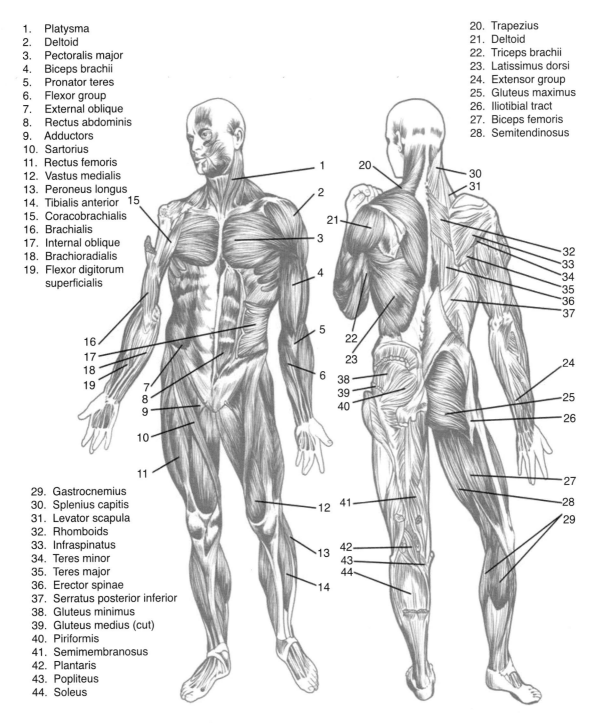

Figure 1.5 The active-muscular system.

The muscles of the body are the powerhouses for all movement and serve as the primary link between the control and passive systems. The interdependent relationship of the active system with both the passive and control systems gives rise to additional terminology that is often used when discussing human movement: The *musculoskeletal system* can be viewed as the interdependent relationship and the combined functions of the passive and active systems. Likewise, the *neuromuscular system* represents the interdependent relationship and combined functions of the control and active systems.

Basic Muscle Function

The unique physiological properties of muscle tissue enable the muscles to respond to the commands sent from the control system and then immediately produce the appropriate pulling forces; these forces are then applied to the levers of the passive system in order to position, stabilize, and move the body. Muscles provide three types of contractile force:

1. *Concentric contraction* occurs when the muscle-tendon unit is shortening while contracting.
2. *Eccentric contraction* occurs when the muscle-tendon unit is producing just enough contractile force to control or slow joint motion while the muscle-tendon unit is lengthening.
3. *Isometric contraction* occurs when the muscle-tendon unit is neither shortening nor lengthening while still producing tension and a contractile force.

Muscles have the highest contractile force potential at or just slightly longer than resting length. Contractile force production is reduced when the muscle length is significantly shortened or lengthened before contraction. This is due to the muscle filaments having little room for additional cross bridging when significantly shortened, or their reduced ability to begin optimal cross bridging when significantly lengthened. Either scenario can be termed as *active insufficiency,* which may be described as a muscle's diminished ability to produce active tension or contractile force. The techniques for each exercise in this book have been modified, particularly in regard to positioning and range of motion, to account for all probable active insufficiency issues at each involved joint.

In addition to their active ability to contract, muscles also have passive elastic properties that enable them to return to their resting length once tension is removed. They also have passive plastic properties that resist being stretched too far. In fact, plastic properties of the muscle fascia can contribute over 40 percent of a joint's level of stiffness or flexibility. With proper active-stretching techniques, some of this resistance can be reduced through safe adaptations of the fascia. Consequently, repetitive forced passive stretching or ballistic stretching can cause deformation of the fascia and damage to the muscle as well as to the connective tissues of the joint. This may result in reduced muscle function and force output, joint instability, or injury. Because of the recommended alignment, positioning, stabilization, and tempo, many of the exercises in this book promote an active stretch for one muscle group as you are targeting an opposing muscle group. These types of exercise selections help to increase mobility or flexibility while also developing stability and strength.

Muscle Actions and Roles

The control system coordinates numerous individual muscle contractions to form muscle synergies that move and stabilize the body in the most efficient manner possible. Depending on the demand, each individual muscle is capable of playing various roles, such as agonists, antagonists, synergists, stabilizers, or neutralizers.

Agonists are muscles that are acting as primary movers for the desired motion. The agonists not only accelerate the concentric movement but also decelerate the eccentric movement; they can also work against the resistance or with the antagonist muscles to produce an isometric contraction. Some muscles are designed to work most often in the role of agonist, antagonist, or synergist to produce joint movement, and these muscles are referred to as *phasic* muscles.

Antagonists are the muscles that work in direct opposition to the concentric movement. To contract any muscle and produce a joint movement, the antagonist muscle must release tension through a controlled action known as *reciprocal inhibition.* Antagonists often play significant "braking" roles when performing fast concentric movements (such as when throwing a ball or swinging a golf club) in order to decelerate the limb or trunk.

Synergists are muscles that assist the agonists or primary movers with the movement. Their angles of attachment at the joint and resulting direction of pull are not as optimal for directly producing the joint movement as those muscles classified as agonists. However, synergists still play important roles in joint motion and stabilization. Their degree of involvement in the joint motion depends on the amount of overall resistance, the direction of resistance, and the present capabilities of the agonists. Synergists often attempt to compensate for agonists that are weak or inhibited. Compensation alters muscle length–tension relationships, decreases joint motion and function, increases joint wear, and can affect posture, gait, and overall movement.

Stabilizers are muscles that are being utilized to isometrically hold a certain joint position or to quasi-isometrically govern the direction and range of joint movement. Some muscles are designed primarily for stabilization or neutralizing roles (such as the postural muscles of the spine and some of the deep core muscles) and are referred to as *tonic* muscles. They are constructed for endurance and have low force output compared to phasic muscles.

Neutralizers are muscles that exert light forces to counteract an unwanted joint motion or force caused by the actions of other muscles. For example, certain core muscles work in concert to neutralize the shearing forces applied to the lumbar spine caused by the forward pull of the psoas to flex the hip during gait movement. Without proper functioning of neutralizers, almost any joint movement would result in mechanical wear and tear on other assisting joints.

Muscular Subsystems

Isolated joint movements may be an important part of a resistance training routine for addressing specific training needs or accomplishing certain goals. However, isolated joint movement rarely occurs in daily life. Therefore, exercise routines should also include multiple-joint movements and general movement patterns that will better train the common muscle synergies or muscular subsystems that are needed to meet life demands.

Since all major body and limb movement is either initiated with trunk movement or preceded by trunk stabilization, the muscular subsystems of the trunk and pelvis should be given the highest priority in training. There are five muscular subsystems that have been identified as critical for trunk and pelvis control:

1. The inner unit (core)
2. The deep longitudinal subsystem (DLS)
3. The lateral subsystem (LS)
4. The posterior oblique subsystem (POS)
5. The anterior oblique subsystem (AOS)

Chapter 2 provides a summary of these subsystems, including their individual components and their associated roles for movement and stabilization of the trunk and pelvis. Illustrations and detailed information related to the manner in which the body depends on these subsystems for production of daily general movement patterns, as well as specific exercise selections that can be used to strengthen these subsystems, will also be presented. This information will be helpful for gaining a better understanding of the exercise selections and the exercise techniques presented in this book.

The Control System

The complexity of the design and inner workings of the entire control or sensorimotor system is far beyond the scope of this book. This section will briefly summarize the basic components of the control system and their associated functions primarily to provide better understanding of the importance of exercise selection and technique. Deeper study of the control system conclusively demonstrates how different exercises will not only train the body in a unique fashion, but will train the entire control-sensorimotor system as well.

The control-sensorimotor system will be viewed as the central nervous system (CNS), peripheral nervous systems, and all sensory receptors that assist with providing information and feedback to the CNS. People receive continual sensory information about their present environment through a number of different sensory channels. A person's three primary sources for sensory information are from visual input, vestibular input, and through proprioception. Proprioception can be generally summed up as input from peripheral sensory receptors and joint mechanoreceptors. Sensory receptors in the skin and cutaneous tissues sense changes in pressure and movement of soft tissue. Mechanoreceptors located in the muscles, joints, and connective tissues give continual information and feedback on joint position, joint stability, joint movement, muscle length, muscle tension, and pressure from external and internal forces.

During any movement, sensory information from all three sources is processed at different levels of the CNS in order to trigger the necessary reflex actions and generate the appropriate motor commands to move, stabilize, and control the body. Motor control is delegated to three general areas of the CNS based on the complexity of the movement and the familiarity of the various stimuli. The three areas are (1) the spinal cord, which handles simple reflex actions; (2) the lower brain, which organizes more complex responses; and (3) the cerebral cortex, which controls the most complicated responses and stores general motor programs. Figure 1.6 depicts these three general control areas and also lists other areas of the control system.

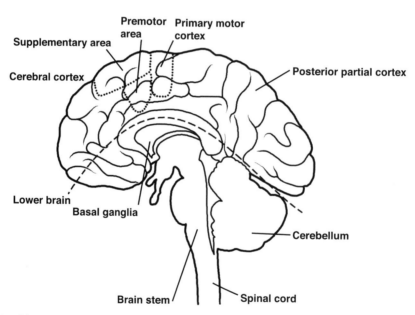

Figure 1.6 Motor control areas of the brain.

The Spinal Cord

The *spinal cord* is made up of two-way tracks of nerve fibers. It carries both sensory fibers as well as motor fibers between the periphery and the brain. The spinal cord allows for the continual flow of afferent information from the sensory receptors to the higher levels of control. It also contains the efferent motor fibers, which carry command information from the cerebrum to the periphery organs or muscles. One branch of the sensory nerves terminates in the gray matter of the spinal cord, while another branch is carried to the higher levels. This enables the spinal cord to react autonomously to certain stimuli without needing any processing or commands from a higher level of control. These reflex actions, such as pulling the hand away from a hot stove or quickly regaining balance after a near fall, are critical for protection and for increasing coordination.

Reflex actions trigger muscle recruitment patterns in a specific manner and can be trained for higher efficiency. However, reflex actions are extremely sensitive to the specific stimulation associated with the movement. Therefore, all aspects of the environment and all elements of technique are important to consider for training reflex actions, because carryover is limited. For example, if a person is training reflex actions for improved balance on an unstable surface (such as a wobble board or an instability disk), transference of these balance improvements to the field or court will be extremely limited. In other words, in reflex training, you generally only get what you specifically train.

The Lower Brain

The *lower brain* consists primarily of the brain stem, the cerebellum, and the basal ganglia. Several descending pathways of motor control are directly or indirectly under the control of the lower brain. Certain afferent sensory information is processed at this level and compared with efferent commands in order to modify a movement for greater efficiency.

The *brain stem* is the stalk of the brain connecting it to the spinal cord and is where all sensory and motor information must pass through. The brain stem is highly involved in maintaining a person's center of gravity, so it plays a significant role in stability training or balance training.

The *cerebellum* attempts to modify all complex movement and is highly involved in ballistic movements such as running, jumping, and agility training. The cerebellum assists the primary motor cortex and the basal ganglia to adjust the actual movement patterns being produced so that they conform to the desired motor patterns established by the higher brain. The cerebellum is always monitoring and modifying movement, so it is highly involved in integrating all specific elements of technique into any exercise.

The *basal ganglia* assist the higher brain with control of complex motor activities. Almost all sensory and motor nerve fibers connecting the cerebral cortex with the spinal cord pass between the basal ganglia. One of the principal responsibilities of the basal ganglia is to initiate and control repetitive and continuous movement patterns such as walking and running.

The Cerebral Cortex

The *cerebral cortex* or higher brain consists of two hemispheres connected by the corpus callosum. The cerebral cortex controls the most complex motor patterns and is responsible for initiation of all voluntary movements. The cerebral cortex has two functional areas concerned with movement, the *motor cortex* and the *somatic sensory cortex*. The cerebral cortex simultaneously processes afferent input from the somatic sensory cortex and coordinates the various activities of the motor cortex with all areas of the lower brain and spinal cord.

The motor cortex is further divided into three basic areas. The *primary motor cortex* helps to control fine voluntary movements and organize reflex actions, the *premotor area* helps to coordinate motor commands and muscle activity, and the *supplementary area* helps with postural adjustments and maintenance of balance.

Together the spinal cord, lower brain, and upper brain—along with the rest of the central nervous system and proprioceptors—are continually attempting to learn, store, recall, and modify movement to help our bodies move and interact within our changing environment more efficiently. The entire control system is constantly being programmed and reprogrammed on a daily basis to adapt not only to changes in the environment but to changes within the active and passive systems as well. As a person grows or shrinks, gains strength or loses strength, and improves or damages working parts, all three systems are affected by these changes and ultimately must be reprogrammed by the control system to integrate improvements or compensate for deficits. This process is continual throughout a person's life and requires constant coordination of the neuromuscular system, which reinforces the need for consistent and efficient exercise.

Neuromuscular Efficiency and Motor Learning

The neuromuscular system can become more synchronized for performing any specific movement or exercise through repeated practice as neuromuscular efficiency is developed. This means the movement can be performed more skillfully with less conscious effort and with less metabolic cost. Improving neuromuscular efficiency, often referred to as *coordination,* is a process because the related systems for improving intermuscular and intramuscular control, increasing reflex activity, and generating faster responses to feedback from afferent receptor information need repeated exposure to the stimuli. Coordination is refined through three basic stages of control as follows:

General Coordination—Cognitive Control   This stage is characterized by the need for cognitive or conscious control of voluntary movement. The individual must think through the movement as it is being performed. The person relies heavily on visual and auditory input because proprioception information is too new and unfamiliar at this stage.

Special Coordination—Associated Control   At this stage, the individual has become more comfortable and begins to feel the proper movements. The person has less reliance on visual and auditory information and more use of proprioception. The person employs stabilization and balance strategies and also begins to utilize feedback information to refine the skill and discard undesired motion.

Specific Coordination—Autonomous Control   This stage is the highest level of motor learning. It is characterized by the performance of the skill through stored motor programs with no conscious thought. The neuromuscular system carries on with automatic reflex actions and response commands to all environmental variables, and the movement pattern is free of all superfluous motion.

General Movement Patterns

An infinite number of possible motor programs could be produced by the human body, which raises the question of how the brain can possibly learn, store, and recall such large amounts of finely detailed data. In answer to this question, Schmidt, among other experts on motor learning, has presented the concept of "generalized motor programs."

Simply stated, this theory proposes that general motor patterns, as opposed to specific, detailed movements, are stored in the higher levels of the brain for quick recall when needed. Then, depending on the afferent information from the various receptors, these general motor programs can be quickly modified at the appropriate level to meet the environmental demands. This storage and recall process is deemed to be most efficient for production and modification of optimal movement. More detailed information pertaining to the development and continued use of general movement patterns—as well as how general movement patterns relate to exercise selection, exercise technique, and exercise program design—will be covered in the following chapters.

Effective Exercise Selection

Before you consider exercise technique, you may need to first analyze your exercise selections. An exercise performed with even the most efficient and safest technique possible will still offer limited value if the exercise was a poor selection for accomplishing the desired goals. In other words, the manner in which each element of technique (such as alignment, positioning, stabilization, motion, tempo, and breathing) is altered should relate to better achievement of the same goals that inspired the selection of the exercise itself.

Appropriate exercise selection is also the key ingredient for designing effective exercise programs. Therefore, since exercise selection is a prerequisite for both exercise technique and exercise programming, this entire chapter is devoted to providing information to help you develop a thought process for safe and efficient exercise selection. This process also integrates the information on anatomical design and function summarized in chapter 1. Exercise selection involves the following four steps, which are detailed in this chapter.

1. Determining goals
2. Targeting desired movement
3. Targeting desired muscle groups
4. Doing benefit-to-risk analysis

Determining Goals

You have numerous goals and desires to consider when selecting any specific exercise. Nearly all benefits of exercise can be categorized into two general areas. One area involves *performance-based goals*. These are goals aimed at benefits that improve the health and functioning of the body but not necessarily the appearance. The other area in which people often seek improvement involves *aesthetic-based goals,* which are those physiological adaptations that make a person look more muscular or fit. Since most people want to obtain some combination of both aesthetic and performance benefits, their exercise programs should include exercises that focus on each of these general goals. It is also possible that certain exercises may address both aesthetic and performance concerns concurrently.

• **Performance-based goals**   Technically, performance-based goals involve the desire for enhancement of *biomotor abilities,* which are the general adaptations or benefits the body can derive from training. They are strength, endurance, stability, mobility, speed, power, and agility. Performance goals include health and wellness concerns such as the desire for general strength gains, improved cardiovascular function, increased joint motion or stability, correction of postural deviations, increased bone density, rehabilitation, or decreased pain. Performance goals may also be related to enhancing athletic abilities such as achieving more specific types of strength, running faster, jumping higher, throwing farther, or improving your golf swing. A large decrease in body fat may also be considered a performance-based goal because it is definitely a health concern. However, fat loss is often related to aesthetic goals as well.

Many performance needs are not necessarily stated goals of the individual. Most people tend to focus on their aesthetic goals and are often not as aware of their diminished levels of physical performance. A medical exam is typically suggested for assisting with determination of health concerns. However, a comprehensive fitness assessment that carefully analyzes joint function and general movement pattern performance is also beneficial for optimally determining a person's performance goals. The comprehensive fitness assessment may also include features such as a postural analysis, gait analysis, and individual joint mobility and stability testing.

• **Aesthetic-based goals**   Aesthetic-based goals relate more to the physiological adaptations that can occur through exercise that affect a person's appearance. Typically, these goals deal primarily with the desire for gains in muscle hypertrophy or muscle size as well as decreases in body fat. However, changes in a person's posture, which would often be categorized as a performance goal, will also dramatically improve the person's appearance. Though fitness professionals today often deemphasize aesthetic goals, these goals are still a driving motivation behind many people's decisions to dedicate the time and energy to an exercise program. Therefore, you should consider and address aesthetic goals when selecting exercises and designing an exercise program.

Targeting Desired Movement

The human body is capable of a vast combination of movement patterns performed in a variety of positions. Therefore, movement is often difficult to classify. The exercise selections and techniques presented in this book are the result of diligent research encompassing anatomy and joint structure, muscle physiology, general physics, biomechanics, neurological processes, and motor learning. Through this complicated process, it was found that exercise movement can be categorized into two types: general movement patterns and specific movement patterns.

General Movement Patterns

General movement patterns (GMPs), as mentioned in chapter 1, maximize the use of the body's designed lever systems and our relative biomechanical advantages to enable us to best move within and interact with our environment. From birth, GMPs develop along with the level of motor control we gain over our bodies. GMPs are typically established by the age of two yet will continue to be modified and refined as our bodies grow and our ability to coordinate movement progresses or declines.

As a person ages, there is an increased tendency for joint wear, joint damage, faulty postural adaptations, and development of muscular imbalances that can begin to deteriorate optimal movement abilities and induce compensatory movement. Compensation eventually further deteriorates joint function to the point where GMPs are extremely limited and daily activity and quality of life are drastically reduced. With these facts in mind, exercise selections that improve or help to restore general movement patterns should be included in almost everyone's exercise program.

General movement patterns are initiated with either spinal movement or spinal stabilization. Once the spine has begun the movement or has been stabilized as the axis for movement, then multiple joint and body movements are possible. From this viewpoint, seven distinct general movement patterns are developed, modified, and repetitively used throughout our lives to best interact with our environment. These seven general movement patterns are as follows:

1. Trunk flexion
2. Trunk extension
3. Trunk rotation
4. Push patterns
5. Pull patterns
6. Squat patterns
7. Gait patterns

You can observe how these movements are developed early in life. Infants first begin to control spinal movement as they learn to flex, extend, and eventually rotate the trunk, while they still have little control over their arms and legs. Later they demonstrate the ability for arm and hand coordination as they begin to perform basic pushing and pulling movements. Then, using combinations of spinal and upper body control, infants learn to crawl and perform assisted squat pattern movements to stand. Eventually children learn to perform varied gait patterns as they begin to walk, run, and climb stairs. General movement patterns progress until a person reaches a certain age and then typically begin to decline as strength, posture, and movement abilities deteriorate.

General movement pattern training not only offers benefits for increased performance but is also the base for pursuing aesthetic goals. GMP exercises are multiple-joint movements that help develop musculature and improve posture through the inclusion of numerous compound movements such as squatting, lunging, pushing, pulling, and various trunk movements. The following sections present the key points for training each of the seven general movement patterns.

Trunk Flexion

Of all spinal movements, forward flexion has the largest degree of available movement. This design allows us to better move and work with our environment directly in front of us (where our eyes, nose, and mouth are located) for efficient interaction between movement and our senses. Muscle action for spinal flexion is performed by the abdominal muscles and obliques. However, since gravity assists with spinal flexion in standing and seated positions, a person rarely has high demands for activation of abdominal and oblique muscles for flexing the spine during normal life activity. In fact, any significant demand on the abdominal and oblique muscles usually comes in an eccentric or isometric role to oppose external forces that attempt to extend or rotate the spine. Therefore, it is wise to select exercises that provide isometric training of spinal flexion along with the exercises that actually produce spinal flexion.

The spine does not flex to the same degree in all regions. Because of the natural kyphotic, or preflexed, position of the thoracic spine, this section typically flexes the greatest degree and with the least resistance. Conversely, because of the natural lordotic or preextended design of the spine in the lumbar and cervical regions, these sections are more difficult to flex. Over time, further decreased ability in lumbar and cervical flexion leads to tightness and often pain in the low back and neck. Therefore, when selecting a resistance training program, include exercises that strengthen lumbar and cervical flexion more than exercises that emphasize thoracic flexion, such as crunches. Figure 2.1 demonstrates exercise selections emphasizing cervical flexion, thoracic flexion, and lumbar flexion.

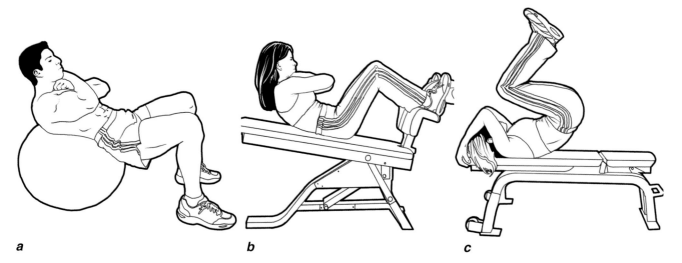

Figure 2.1   Exercise selections targeting *(a)* cervical flexion, *(b)* thoracic flexion, and *(c)* lumbar flexion.

Trunk Extension

Extension of the spine is naturally limited by design in the middle region or thoracic spine (which is the largest region). This limitation can also be considered an advantage when it comes to resisting extension forces attempting to bend the spine backward. However, because of the preextended positioning of the lumbar and cervical regions of the spine, these areas are at risk for *hyperextension* when working against extension forces, such as during standing presses or push-ups, and also when performing active trunk extension movements. Therefore, movements that promote thoracic extension along with lumbar and cervical stabilization are the primary extension exercises presented in this book. Thoracic extension can also be trained isometrically along with extension of the lumbar spine during numerous back and leg exercises, such as bent-over rowing, squats, or barbell hip extensions. Figure 2.2 compares static trunk extensor stabilization to dynamic trunk extension.

Figure 2.2   Compare *(a)* static trunk extension with *(b)* dynamic trunk extension.

Trunk Rotation

The most difficult and riskiest spinal movements are those that emphasize trunk rotation. This is because safe degrees of rotation at any one vertebral joint are limited. There are 26 possible articulation points for spinal rotation. Each joint has a varying degree of optimal movement ability that contributes to the overall degree of spinal rotation. The rotation ability of the spine is limited in the lumbar section but immediately increases in the thoracic section, with even more rotation possible in the cervical section. A limitation in one of the vertebral joints will trigger compensation and possible excess rotation in other vertebral joints in an attempt to maintain the overall amount of spinal rotation. This compensatory movement stresses muscles along with connective tissue and begins to degenerate vertebral discs. This eventually results in further limited movement at certain sections with accompanying increased compensation at others.

In short, optimal rotation of the spine is a complicated biomechanical process involving numerous musculoskeletal and neuromuscular components that are difficult to observe, so this movement must be trained cautiously. Limited spinal rotation often cannot be corrected by simply performing rotational exercises. In fact, aggressive training of rotational exercises may only induce further compensation and promote further degeneration and injury. A qualified doctor, therapist, or highly skilled trainer should assess rotational movement ability before you select aggressive rotational movements. Lumbar flexion, cervical flexion, and thoracic extension should all be well developed before attempting aggressive rotational movements of the spine. Selection of exercises that statically stabilize against trunk rotation is an alternative option to dynamic rotational movements for strengthening the muscular subsystems responsible for spinal rotation. Figure 2.3 compares these two options.

a   b

Figure 2.3 Compare (a) static spinal rotation with (b) dynamic spinal rotation.

Push Patterns

The production of any movement is the result of muscles pulling on the bony levers of the skeleton. Therefore, all muscles pull and there are technically no pushing muscles. To create a push pattern, a person must combine two or more muscle pulls that collectively produce a pushing force to be applied against the ground or an object. Lower body push patterns are classified as either squat or gait movements, both of which are covered in later sections of this chapter.

Upper body push patterns directly involve varying degrees of scapular, shoulder, elbow, and wrist movement. You should also consider stabilization requirements of the trunk and lower body when selecting pushing exercises. Because human movement is described within a three-plane system, people typically use exercise movements that are primarily contained within one of these three planes. When selecting pushing exercises, consider exercises that produce movement in all three planes and in between each plane as well. You can select single-arm push patterns or pressing with offset loads for each arm to provide different stabilization demands or to target specific subsystems. Figure 2.4 provides examples of pushing patterns performed in the three defined planes of motion.

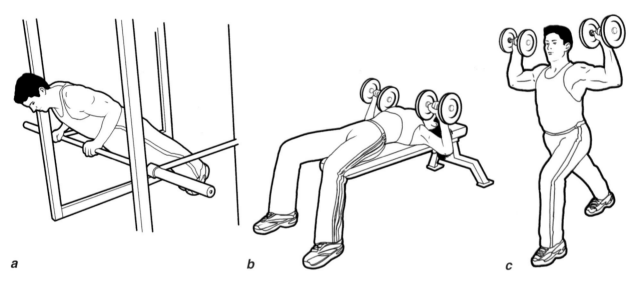

a   *b*   *c*

Figure 2.4 Pushing patterns: *(a)* on the median plane, *(b)* on the horizontal plane, and *(c)* on the frontal plane.

Pull Patterns

As previously stated, all muscles pull, so technically any movement could be considered a pulling movement. Pull patterns are movements that incorporate two or more joint movements to produce a combined force that either pulls an object toward the body or pulls the body toward the object. Both are similar actions but do train the pulling musculature differently. Pulling patterns involve varying degrees of scapular, shoulder, elbow, and wrist motion, and they are critical movements for developing postural muscles of the spine.

Pulling patterns target the back and spinal extensors, but they can also challenge the lower body and certain muscular subsystems depending on the exercise positioning selected. Pulling in each plane of movement requires unique timing and certain degrees of scapular-humeral rhythm that will emphasize different pulling muscles. For most people who are free from shoulder, scapular, and spinal injuries, pulling exercises for all three planes and even pulling movements between planes should be included in a resistance training program. Unilateral, or single-arm, pulling will also present different stabilization demands on the body and apply additional rotational forces to the spine that will require additional action of the trunk muscles. Figure 2.5 shows examples of different pulling movements occurring in the three defined planes, each of which accomplishes different goals or addresses different needs.

Squat Patterns

The squat pattern is one of the most basic and functional movements that humans use for accomplishing numerous daily tasks. Sitting and rising from a chair, picking up and setting down a box, or squatting and holding the position for a prolonged period in order to retrieve a file from a drawer are all common examples of squat patterns. Yet in the typical exercise

Figure 2.5 Pulling movements: *(a)* on the median plane, *(b)* on the horizontal plane, and *(c)* on the frontal plane.

program prescribed today, the squat is often one of the first exercises to be eliminated or overlooked because of the perceived risks with the exercise. The squat itself is rarely a high-risk movement for most people, even those with back or knee problems. The real risk with the squat is usually associated with the technique that has been learned or the manner and amount of loading.

The specific elements of technique—such as the alignment, positioning, range of movement, stabilization, and tempo—are more important variables associated with the relative risk of the squat than the amount of resistance selected. Squat patterns in life are varied, and the squat patterns within an exercise program should also be varied. Also, since load placement and amounts vary in life, so again should they be varied with exercise selection. Figure 2.6 demonstrates optional squat exercises that can help people accomplish different goals or address different needs. Specifics on technique for such exercises are described in chapter 5.

Figure 2.6 Squat exercises: *(a)* dumbbell deadlift (wide-stance squat), *(b)* barbell moderate-stance squat, and *(c)* barbell deadlift (narrow-stance squat).

Gait Patterns

Gait is the manner in which we translate or move our bodies across the surface of our environment. In other words, gait is the way we travel using the body's own means. Gait is typically pictured as walking but could include an endless number of variations, such as skipping, hopping, walking sideways, or even walking backward. Several gait modifications deal with different demands or achieve different goals; therefore, there are numerous choices in agility and resistance exercise for training modified gait motions. However, for the purposes of this book, we discuss only those variations that people use most often and how this relates to selection of resistance exercise.

If normal walking is considered to be gait, then the first variation to take into account is how gait is modified as leg speed and body speed increase. Walking eventually becomes running, which calls for a distinctly different timing and degree of trunk, hip, knee, ankle, and even arm movements. Body lean is slightly increased and foot strike is altered as a person moves from walking to running. As speed continues to increase, another distinct modification to gait takes place, again requiring different timing and different degrees of body and limb movements as a person moves from running to sprinting. Forward lean of the body again increases, and heel or foot strike is transformed to toe strike. Obviously, these common gait variations can be easily trained in a fitness program, if appropriate for the person, by simply including periodic walking, running, and sprinting workouts.

Another common but often overlooked gait variation occurs when the body needs to modify normal gait because of a change in angle of movement (as opposed to a change in speed of movement). Moving over different ground elevations, such as walking up stairs or stagger-stepping down a hill, demands as much modification to normal gait as running or sprinting does. When training these common gait variations, lunging, reverse lunging, or step-up type exercises are challenging and useful exercise selections for the program. Figure 2.7 demonstrates the most common variations to gait.

Weakness of a muscular subsystem or individual joint can induce compensation and alter any desired gait movement. When this occurs, attempting to improve gait movement by simply practicing the desired movement does not increase performance; rather, it only reinforces compensation. Improvements in gait will often require specific resistance training exercises that strengthen weak subsystems or individual joints in order to correct existing muscular imbalances and joint dysfunctions. Certain therapies and medical intervention may also be needed for treating serious joint dysfunctions that hinder normal gait movement.

Gait analysis is a complex topic, and it is not within the scope of this book to venture into this field in depth. However, understanding the basic phases of gait and how they correlate to muscular subsystem action will be helpful in exercise selection for improvement of any variation in desired gait. Specific exercises target the specific subsystem that dominates each phase of gait. The three general phases of gait and the dominant subsystems responsible for the associated gait actions are as follows (these subsystems are further summarized in the next section of this chapter):

1. Propulsion phase—Posterior oblique subsystem (POS)
2. Stance phase—Deep longitudinal subsystem (DLS) and lateral subsystem (LS)
3. Swing phase—Anterior oblique subsystem (AOS)

Figure 2.7 Gait variations: *(a)* walking, *(b)* running, *(c)* sprinting, and *(d)* lunging.

Specific Movement Patterns

Specific movement patterns are multijoint or individual-joint movements that may be selected in a resistance training program to address specific performance-based goals or help to accomplish certain aesthetic-based goals. Since most people have both performance and aesthetic goals, it is logical that most resistance training programs would include specific movement patterns as well as general movement patterns. The specific movement patterns presented in this book can be used to address many common performance-based goals, and some are designed to achieve general aesthetic-based goals. However, some athletes may also wish to include complementary movement patterns, such as Olympic lifting movements, plyometric exercises, or speed and agility training, designed to address certain goals related to their sport performance.

Targeting Desired Muscle Groups

When you select any exercise movement, you are also inevitably choosing to target specific muscles and muscular subsystems, whether or not it is a conscious choice. Exercise selection based on targeting movement patterns and based on targeting muscles should be part of the same thought process because they go hand in hand. People selecting exercises for performance-based goals may be more focused on the movement, whereas people looking for exercises to accomplish aesthetic-based goals tend to focus more on the muscle groups. When you are attempting to target the muscles, the choices will again be divided into two general categories. You can choose to target muscular synergies, or subsystems, or you can choose to target specific muscle groups and isolated muscle actions.

Muscular Subsystems

The control system rarely recruits individual muscles but rather recruits muscle synergies in order to stabilize and move the body or limbs. As previously mentioned, all major body and limb movement is initiated through spinal movement or preceded by spinal stabilization. Therefore, the muscular synergies, or subsystems, that control spinal and pelvic movement should be given the highest priority for training. Five subsystems have been identified as critical components for performance of trunk movement and for trunk stabilization: the inner unit (core), the deep longitudinal subsystem (DLS), the lateral subsystem (LS), the posterior oblique subsystem (POS), and the anterior oblique subsystem (AOS).

Inner Unit (Core)

Several authors have cited research on spinal segmental stabilization that has clearly identified a local stabilizing system known as the inner unit. This deep collection of abdominal, pelvic, and spinal musculature performs dual functions for both respiration and stabilization. The inner unit, or "core," is uniquely designed to accomplish both tasks simultaneously. The inner unit is under separate neurological control and can function independently from the outer trunk muscles such as the rectus abdominis, the external obliques, and the larger erector spinae. The inner unit is highly involved in spinal and pelvic stability but relies on the outer layers of trunk and spinal muscle for performing actual trunk movements.

The core is composed of superior, inferior, anterior, and posterior muscles that enclose the contents of the abdominal cavity or *viscera*. The core muscles help to provide intra-abdominal pressure to stabilize the spine while still performing respiratory functions. The primary muscles of the core are the diaphragm, the pelvic floor muscles, the transverse abdominis, and the deep spinal muscles collectively known as the transversospinalis group. However, deep lower spinal muscles, such as the posterior fibers of the internal obliques and the quadratus lumborum, assist with pelvic-lumbar stability and are also considered by some authors as part of the core.

As the core muscles provide for critical spinal intersegmental control and "local" spinal stabilization, larger trunk muscles such as the rectus abdominis, spinal erectors, obliques, and even certain hip muscles work as "global" spinal stabilizers and provide the force needed for actual trunk or hip movement. Some authors also include these muscles as part of the core, but they are listed simply as trunk or hip muscles in this book.

The transverse abdominis as well as other core and trunk muscles attach to the spine through a large, broad, and flattened tendon called the *thoracolumbar aponeurosis* (also known as the *thoracolumbar fascia*). The thoracolumbar fascia is a network of noncontractile tendonlike tissue laid out in anterior, middle, and posterior layers. It is a critical component of the core and plays a vital role in spinal stabilization. It also acts as a force transference mechanism for the various muscular subsystems of the body.

The Core and Respiration   The core's ability to simultaneously perform its dual roles (assisting with respiration while providing spinal stabilization) is more dependent on the breathing method than on any other element of technique. The breathing method presented in this book is based on the core mechanics involved in assisting with inhalation and exhalation while also providing local spinal stabilization. The core's specific actions related to respiration will be described in the following sections. Integration of this information as a part of exercise technique through application of a specific breathing method is presented in chapter 3.

Inhalation   The diaphragm is a dome-shaped muscle that originates along the lower ribs and inserts along the anterior surfaces on the lower thoracic and lumbar spine. If unrestricted, the diaphragm initiates inhalation and helps the lungs begin to draw in air and expand the thoracic cavity by creating a downward push on the contents of the abdominal cavity or viscera. This downward force increases intra-abdominal pressure and pushes the viscera down against the bowl of the pelvis. This in turn signals a co-contraction of the pelvic floor muscles, which assists with stabilization of the pelvic and sacral joints. Visceral pressure also signals a co-contraction of the multifidi and other transversospinalis muscles, which assists in stabilizing the lower and middle levels of the spine. The increased intra-abdominal pressure also begins to cause the viscera to distend forward, creating passive tension from the transverse abdominis and a tightening of the thoracolumbar fascia, which further stabilizes the pelvis and creates a stiffening of the spine.

A concert of spinal and costal muscles completes inhalation by expanding and slightly elevating the rib cage. This action further extends the thoracic spine and results in a straightened and improved posture. At full inhalation, both the abdominal and thoracic cavities are pressurized, and there are high levels of muscular support for stabilization of optimal posture. At this point, by simply holding the breath and tightening the outer abdominal muscles, a person can perform what is known as the *Valsalva maneuver,* which provides for maximal stability of the spine. The Valsalva maneuver is a natural protective mechanism that is also often initiated automatically when a person's balance or spinal stability is suddenly challenged. Though it provides immediate and maximal support for stabilizing posture, longer-term use of the Valsalva maneuver (for more than several seconds) has associated risks because it tends to increase blood pressure and deprive the body tissues of oxygen. Therefore, you should understand the roles of the core muscles in, and incorporate methods for, exhalation as well as inhalation. Figure 2.8 depicts core muscle actions for inhalation.

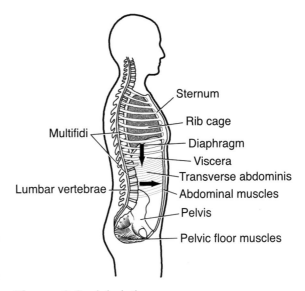

Figure 2.8   Inhalation.

Exhalation   The greater challenge for spinal and postural stabilization occurs when exhaling as pressure is being lost from both the abdominal and thoracic cavities. However, through a contraction of the transverse abdominis, this pressure loss is minimized and core activation is increased to assist with continued stabilization. The contraction of the transverse abdominis creates a drawing in of the viscera, much like the tightening of a wide belt, and presses the viscera back, down, and upward, which maintains greater levels of intra-abdominal and intrathoracic pressure. This pressure coupled with co-contractions of the pelvic floor muscles, transversospinalis muscles, and deep erector muscles, along with a reciprocal relaxation of the diaphragm, helps to maintain spinal and pelvic stabilization while assisting with exhalation (see figure 2.9).

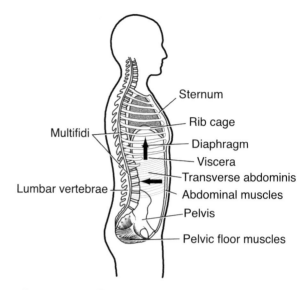

Figure 2.9 Exhalation.

Research confirms that some of these core muscles are the first muscles to be recruited for any major body or limb movement as well as respiration. Control of intra-abdominal pressure also appears to be an automated action of the core muscles that provides for the lower levels of stabilization needed for most daily activities. However, it is also believed that these automated actions can become inhibited through injury, surgery, immune system stress, disease, or perhaps through faulty exercise and breathing techniques. Also consider the fact that resistance training frequently includes working with heavier loads for more challenging and repetitive movements than those typically encountered in daily activities. For both reasons, it is important to incorporate specific core activation and breathing methods as an element of technique.

Compensation can result from faulty breathing techniques and can cause the development of muscular imbalances and postural deviations. For example, restricting the initial action of the diaphragm through an overemphasis of constant transverse abdominal activation will often induce compensational actions of the scalenes, levator scapula, and other muscles of the cervical spine in an attempt to further elevate the rib cage for achieving greater lung volume. This in turn alters cervical spine positioning and increases mechanical wear. Nerve and vascular structures can also become restricted, leading to muscular dysfunction and reduced blood flow to the upper extremities.

Deep Longitudinal Subsystem (DLS)

The DLS helps to stabilize the body from ankle to head. It also provides for reciprocal force transmission from the ground to the trunk and back down. The DLS includes the tibialis anterior, the peroneus longus, the biceps femoris, the sacrotuberous ligament, the erector spinae, and the thoracolumbar fascia. The major roles of the subsystem are to absorb and transfer ground force, stabilize the ankle, decelerate forward leg movement, and stabilize the spine by resisting trunk flexion. The DLS is dominant in the stance phase of gait and is triggered as the heel strikes the ground as pictured in figure 2.10.

As the leg moves forward during the swing phase when walking or running, the hamstring muscles activate just enough to decelerate the forward leg movement or hip flexion and knee extension. The activation

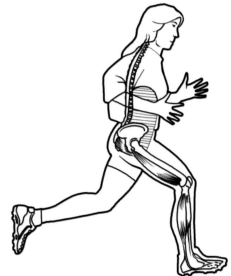

Figure 2.10 The deep longitudinal subsystem.

of the biceps femoris increases tension in the sacrotuberous ligament, which transfers force across the sacrum, stabilizing the sacroiliac joint of the pelvis, and allows for force transference up through the erector spinae to help stabilize the trunk. The tightening of the biceps femoris also causes tension through the peroneus longus, which works in concert with the tibialis anterior to stabilize the ankle in preparation for the heel to strike the ground. The DLS then captures kinetic energy resulting from the heel strike via the thoracolumbar fascia and transfers these forces to the posterior oblique system for the propulsion phase of gait.

Lateral Subsystem (LS)

The LS works with the DLS to stabilize for impact but does so from the frontal plane. It is composed primarily of the hip abductor musculature (gluteus medius, gluteus minimus, tensor fasciae latae) and the contralateral or opposite-side trunk lateral flexors (quadratus lumborum, internal obliques), with some assisting control from the ipsilateral or same-side hip adductors. The LS is most involved in the stance phase of gait; pelvic and spinal stabilization during single-leg impact highly relies on this subsystem. The LS is depicted in action in figure 2.11. As the man presses sideways off the stationary leg, the hip abductors work with the opposite-side lateral flexors of the trunk to stabilize the pelvis and also to provide a slight hip lift of the opposite leg. This action helps to balance the body's shifted center of gravity and also provides for optimal positioning needed for the succeeding impact of the opposite leg, which in turn would signal immediate activation of the opposite-side LS.

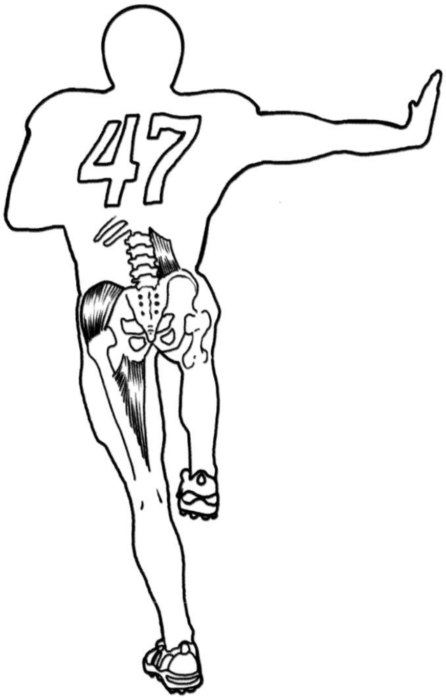

Figure 2.11 The lateral subsystem.

Gait movements that involve accelerated side-to-side motion for sports such as football, speedskating, or tennis rely heavily on strong and well-synchronized lateral subsystems. Several resistance training exercises would target the LS directly as the primary stabilization subsystem.

Posterior Oblique Subsystem (POS)

The POS is composed primarily of the latissimus dorsi and the contralateral or opposite-side gluteus maximus. The POS works synergistically with the DLS through transference of kinetic energy across their shared attachments into the thoracolumbar fascia. The POS is demonstrated during normal gait movement in figure 2.12.

As the leg moves forward in the swing phase of gait, the ipsilateral gluteus maximus of the POS assists the hamstrings to decelerate hip flexion, while the contralateral latissimus dorsi activates to decelerate forward flexion or swing of the opposite arm. There is a parallel alignment of the muscle fibers of the gluteus maximus and the contralateral latissimus dorsi. They run diagonally across the sacroiliac joint, which helps to stabilize the pelvis during the impact of heel strike and prepares the entire lumbar-pelvic region for propulsion.

Though involved in deceleration of the arm and opposite leg during swing phase, the POS is most dominant in the propulsion phase of gait. The POS uses stored kinetic energy transferred through the thoracolumbar fascia to accelerate opposite hip and shoulder extension, which helps to push off the ground and propel the body forward. The timing of the co-contraction of the POS produces tension that assists with continued pelvic and lumbar stabilization and can be stored for use in the following phases of gait. The POS is also of prime importance in rotational actions, such as swinging a bat or golf club or throwing a baseball, because it cocks the body before rotation, then decelerates the body after rotation has begun.

Anterior Oblique Subsystem (AOS)

The AOS works similarly to the POS but from an anterior orientation. The AOS is composed primarily of the adductors of the hip with their ipsilateral or same-side internal obliques and the contralateral or opposite-side external obliques. The hip adductors work with the contralateral obliques through the parallel alignment of their fibers and the close proximity of attachment at the pubis, which facilitates force transference and communication between the two muscle groups. The AOS is pictured in figure 2.13 as its actions are being demonstrated during a general gait movement.

The AOS is dominant in the swing phase of gait as the hip adductors and contralateral trunk rotators work synergistically to stabilize the body on top of the stance leg while rotating the pelvis for the forward swing of the back leg. The AOS also works closely with the POS to time and blend the propulsion and swing phases of gait while also providing for optimal positioning of the pelvis and leg to prepare for impact on the succeeding heel strike of the opposite leg.

The AOS is also dominant during acceleration in rotational movements such as when throwing objects or swinging implements. This subsystem would be a priority for strengthening (along with balanced POS training) for anyone involved in sports requiring a high volume or high intensity of throwing, swinging, or punching.

In addition to these deep subsystems of the trunk, other common muscle synergies should be trained in any resistance training program. The muscle synergies that should be given the next-highest priority are those that are needed most often for performance of daily life movements. These muscle synergies correspond directly to the seven general movement patterns previously discussed. Therefore, by selecting exercises that flex, extend, and rotate the spine as well as push, pull, squat, and strengthen gait movement, people will automatically train the muscle synergies most needed to address the performance needs and achieve the aesthetic goals they may have.

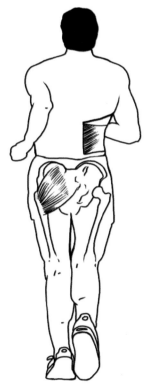

Figure 2.12 The posterior oblique subsystem.

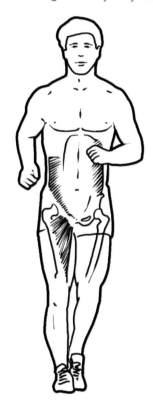

Figure 2.13 The anterior oblique subsystem.

Specific Muscle Isolation

For the same reasons that people target specific movement patterns, they may also want to select certain exercises that isolate specific muscles. Targeting specific muscles in an isolated manner is often necessary in order to address a performance need and correct muscular imbalances. These exercises often include isolated strengthening of the rotator cuff and shoulder girdle, hip and pelvic-lumbar stabilization, as well as wrist, elbow, ankle, and knee musculature. Some of these types of specific exercise movements are included within this book, but many more that may complement them can be found in books focused on rehabilitation or physical therapy.

Another reason that people may want to isolate certain muscles is associated with aesthetic goals. Numerous exercises and machines have been designed for the sole purpose of isolating a specific muscle in order to influence its size and shape. Volumes of books have been filled with isolated exercises that are intended to help people develop and build the chest, back, shoulders, arms, and legs. Some of these types of exercises are included in this book, whereas many others have intentionally been excluded. Exercises that encourage heavy loading of isolated joint motions, particularly those exercises that target shoulder musculature, often have too high a risk for damage compared to the potential benefits for many people.

Determining Risk Versus Benefit of Resistance Exercise

For a movement of any joint to take place, there must be a directive force, and the transference of forces needs to occur. As any joint receives and transfers forces, there is always an inherent risk of damage to the joint as well as the opportunity to gain desired benefits. So any resistance training exercise may offer perceived benefits, but it will also have some ratio of potential risk involved. The risk may not be fully known but is always present, whereas the benefit may be perceived and not always actual. Therefore, a person should always strive to maximize actual and real benefits and decrease all present risks involved with any exercise selection.

To fully understand the potential risk or benefits associated with any exercise, a person would have to research a tremendous amount of information associated with the physics of the movement itself, in-depth structural analysis of each involved joint, and all the associated physiological and biomechanical issues involved. A compilation of all this information was considered in the selection of the exercises and techniques in this book. However, not every exercise presented in the book is appropriate for every person's goals. When selecting exercises from any source, consider the following guidelines to reduce the risk and potentially increase the benefits.

- Goal identification. Be sure the movement pattern, whether general or specific, matches the movement you wish to improve. Confirm the exercise is actually targeting the muscles or subsystems you wish to target.

- Alignment and positioning. There are numerous options in alignment and positioning for performing any resistance training movement. Be sure the alignment and positioning are appropriate to your goals and match your present abilities to stabilize the selected options. If not, consider appropriate modifications.

- Movement control. Many aspects of the movements are also optional, particularly when it comes to the range and speed of motion. If the range of motion takes any joints of the body to positions they could not achieve naturally, you should reduce the range of movement. If the movement speed results in a loss of the ability to stabilize the desired alignment and positioning, you should reduce the speed.

- Breathing. The maintenance of a regular breathing technique and tempo works synergistically to assist with all other elements of technique. If breathing becomes restricted or sporadic during any resistance training exercise, potential risk may increase. A breathing method is presented in this book as a part of overall technique that may help to reduce any risk associated with inefficient breathing.

These guidelines to help increase the benefits and decrease the risks are simply the application of the identified elements of technique presented in this book. The following chapter discusses each element of technique in detail, and it describes how these elements independently and collectively help to improve the efficiency and benefits as well as decrease the risks of any exercise they are applied to.

Optimal Exercise Technique

To make any exercise as efficient and as safe as possible, the specific exercise technique used is the most critical variable. I chose the word *variable* because opinions and philosophies are abundant related to resistance training technique. Several elements make up exercise technique, and the way these elements are viewed and varied will dictate the overall performance of an exercise. Many resistance exercise techniques presented today were developed in the gym through trial-and-error methods. They were designed based on predetermined goals such as the desire to gain more muscle mass or move heavier weight loads. Functional anatomy, actual biomechanics, or even simple physics were rarely taken into account in the early developmental years of resistance training.

The human body accomplishes movement through the coordination of highly integrated and interdependent systems. Muscles are not designed for aesthetic appearance but rather for mechanical function. To control our bodies and interact within our environment, the active-muscular system carries on two-way communication with the control-sensorimotor system in order to move or stabilize the passive-skeletal system. All three systems work continually to increase the efficiency of movement and decrease compensation and metabolic cost. Each exercise movement a person performs not only affects the body's "hardware" but also programs the "software" for better coordination and future performance. This is why exercise technique is so important to consider. Manipulation of any element of technique will invariably increase or decrease efficiency and affect the level of risk associated with the overall movement.

Seven distinct elements of exercise technique can be varied or manipulated to better achieve certain goals or address specific needs:

1. Goal identification
2. Exercise motion
3. Alignment
4. Positioning
5. Stabilization

6. Tempo

7. Breathing

These interdependent elements will first be discussed individually to help you appreciate how they relate to each other and how they can be combined to establish an overall technique for any resistance training exercise. The more you understand these critical elements of exercise technique, the better you will become at identifying, manipulating, and varying them for any exercise.

Goal Identification

Clearly identifying the goal is probably the most important element of technique and should be done before selecting the exercise itself. The same goals that inspired the exercise selection will also affect all other elements of technique. Modifications in the movement, tempo, alignment, positioning, and stabilization strategies will often need to be made in order to best accomplish the desired goals. However, no matter what the goal, when modifications to the technique of an exercise are made, all biomechanical factors must still be considered, and the technique must be kept within the anatomical limits and control abilities of the person performing the exercise. In other words, the pursuit of a training goal should never necessitate a resistance training exercise or technique that compromises the safety of the individual.

Exercises selected for performance-based goals typically apply different technique options than similar exercises selected for aesthetic-based goals. This is because there is an entirely different thought process for selecting exercises and modifying techniques to accomplish performance-based goals versus aesthetic-based goals. Table 3.1 compares the two types of goals in respect to certain elements of technique.

The amount of proprioceptive activity, or sensory input, and the specific neurological demands of an exercise are related to the selected technique, particularly the alignment, positioning, and stabilization options chosen for any exercise. Table 3.1 makes it clear that performance-based goals typically lead to exercise and technique selections that contain more neurological demand and provide higher proprioceptive activity. Training the body in fixed movement patterns and when externally stabilized may help build bigger muscles but typically offers little transference for addressing most performance goals. Conversely, these same exercise selections and technique options may be ideal for achieving certain aesthetic goals. Since most people have a mixture of goals, it would be prudent to include different exercises that utilize techniques for accomplishing both. Chapter 9 provides some examples of exercise routines that address both performance needs and aesthetic goals.

TABLE 3.1   Training Goals and Exercise Technique

Goal	Focus	Motion	Alignment and positioning	Stabilization	Proprioception and neural demand
Performance-based goals	Enhancing muscular performance	Unrestricted, often unilateral	Varied, asymmetrical	More self-supported	High proprioception, high neural demand
Aesthetic-based goals	Enhancing muscular size	Specified, often bilateral	Consistent, symmetrical	More environment-supported	Low proprioception, high neural availability

Exercise Motion

The element of technique that probably varies the most in resistance training is the exercise motion itself. The exercise motion dictates the use of all individual joints, the recruitment of all involved muscles, and the specific motor patterns to be learned. Therefore, the type, path, range, and speed (or tempo) of motion are all critical factors of exercise technique.

Type and Path of Motion

Only four types of movement can be attributed to any object, or in other words four pathways through which an object may travel. Therefore, human movement can be specified according to these four classifications.

Rotatory motion is the movement of an object or segment around a fixed axis in a circular path. For the purposes of this book, any isolated joint movement will be considered a rotatory movement. Isolated rotatory motion is sometimes prescribed to isolate individual muscles for specific performance goals, but it is more commonly selected to accomplish aesthetic or body-building goals. Isolated rotatory joint motion exercises do not directly transfer to life demands, and they can also place high stress on the joint and increase mechanical wear if intensity or volume becomes too high. Therefore, you should consider using conservative weight loads and reduced volume with this type of movement.

Translatory or *linear motion* is the movement of an object or segment in a fixed or linear path. Since all individual joints are rotational, they cannot produce linear motion without the co-commitment of another joint. Even then, the human body does not produce true linear movement very efficiently. Therefore, performing exercises in a fixed linear path—such as when training on a Smith machine, leg press sled, or hack squat machine—tends to produce translatory forces across the joints, resulting in additional shear of joint surfaces. When choosing exercises that produce linear movement, it is best if they are performed with free weights or cables that do not restrict the path of movement.

Curvilinear motion is the combination of rotatory and linear motion. Technically, since no joint of the body is completely rounded or flat, all human joint motion is curvilinear. As the joint rotates over or glides along bony articular surfaces, slight shifts in the axis result in a curvilinear movement of the distal end of the segment. However, since the shifts are often slight, individual joint movements are most often classified as rotatory movement.

General plane motion is described as the rotatory or curvilinear movement of a segment around an axis that is also in movement in the same plane. Most of our traditional exercises have been taught and performed in one general plane of motion, whether they are single-joint isolated movements or multiple-joint compound movements. The human body is also typically classified as having three general planes of movement as pictured in figure 1.4 in chapter 1.

Obviously, the body has undefined movement between planes and movements that can take place in multiple planes. Though multiple-plane movement is a part of many daily activities, there is a risk in attempting to perform multiple-plane movements when loaded. If performing multiple-plane resistance training exercises, be sure to select a weight that is appropriate for the muscles controlling the most challenging part of the movement. The exception for this guideline may be when performing certain power exercises such as a hang clean. With proper technique, momentum will carry the load through the most challenging portion of the movement and dramatically reduce the demand on the weakest muscles in the kinetic chain.

The type and path of motion should be specific and predetermined in accordance with achieving the goal. With performance-based goals, the movement itself is often more of the focus than the muscles that produce the movement. Therefore, the type and path of motion must match the movement pattern that has been targeted for improvement. However, the type and path of motion will also be important in order to best target and properly load specific muscles that have been targeted to accomplish an aesthetic goal. In short, the type and path of motion should be carefully selected for best accomplishing the specific training goals of the individual.

Range of Motion

One of the most debated issues in resistance training is the difference of opinion concerning range of motion. It has been traditionally believed that training with a "full" range of motion (ROM) brings about the most benefits for muscle and joint performance. The problem with this philosophy is determining what "full" actually means. Some people perceive the ROM as being determined by how far the bar or weight load moves and give little thought to body movement, alignment, or positioning. This view often leads to drastically different ranges of actual joint motion for one person to complete the prescribed ROM versus another person with different limb lengths. This is why there is no one set range of motion for any resistance exercise. For this book, ROM has been prescribed based on safe and efficient levels of actual joint motion for most healthy people. ROM is described by amounts of body movement, never by bar, machine, or weight movement. ROM may need to be further modified for those individuals with prior injury, joint damage, or preexisting conditions.

Several factors affect the range of motion of an exercise. Anatomical and musculoskeletal structure, physics and force transferences, neurological or sensorimotor control, and the specific training goals could all have an influence on determining ROM for any exercise. To stay within the focus of this book, this section summarizes only the natural anatomical limits to joint motion that are often overlooked but should be considered as a part of exercise technique.

The bones themselves limit range of motion by design. Their unique shapes and bony prominences allow for certain degrees of movement in some directions while restricting motion in other directions. For example, the shallow concave shape of the glenoid fossa (shoulder socket) allows for a great amount of motion for the attached humerus. It is by far the most mobile joint on the human body and gives us an extreme amount of possible movement patterns in all three planes. However, once movements are combined, such as internal rotation with abduction, ROM is drastically reduced. In fact, performing exercises with this shoulder positioning (such as upright rows or steep decline presses) may impinge and injure certain connective tissue, musculature, and the bursa if the ROM is not appropriately modified.

ROM of one joint is often dependent on prior or synergistic movement of another joint. For example, the same shoulder joint just discussed can typically abduct 180 degrees if it is externally rotated before this movement and if the movement is combined with upward rotation of the scapula. Therefore, when performing an exercise that requires this motion, prior shoulder positioning, force alignment, spinal stabilization, and proper scapular-humeral rhythm must all be monitored to safely achieve the desired ROM.

The study of bony surfaces as well as their shapes can also lead to making wiser selections for exercise range of motion. The location and thickness of articular cartilage on bone surfaces provide information on where and how far motion is designed to travel. For example, study of articular cartilage of the hip shows that loaded flexion and extension of the femur are more suited for this joint when in a standing position (such as when squatting) than when performing a similar action in a flexed hip position (such as when seated performing a leg press). Articular cartilage is critical for joint health and is not easily replaced, so ROM should be carefully prescribed for such exercises, and weight loads should perhaps be limited.

ROM is also limited by joint structure. A joint of the body is the meeting place of two or more bones. Bones are held together by ligaments, and muscles attach to bones via their tendons. The elasticity of ligaments and tendons is low because they are not designed to stretch; rather, they are designed to stabilize and control joint movement. Any significant stretching of a ligament or tendon may begin to tear or deform it, thereby reducing its ability to optimally stabilize and control the joint.

Another component of the joint that affects ROM is the joint capsule. Although joint capsules have more elasticity than ligaments or tendons, they also have plastic characteristics that help to stabilize the joint and to transfer forces from a working muscle to the adjacent bone. This means that joint capsules are also at risk for damage with ROM outside their designed limits. ROM capabilities of the capsule, ligaments, and tendons are predetermined by their structure. Research suggests that almost half of the mobility at any joint is determined by the genetic structure of these connective tissues. In other words, some people are born with more joint ROM capabilities (flexibility) than others, just as some people are born with more muscular force potential (strength) than others.

Muscles themselves can also limit ROM in several ways. One way is known as *active insufficiency,* which is the diminished capacity of a muscle to produce active tension once shortened or lengthened too far. Therefore, if targeting a certain muscle is part of the goal of an exercise, then the ROM of the movement should be kept within the limits of where the muscle is able to maintain active tension and produce force. This is particularly true for muscles that cross over two or more joints, because they are more prone to active insufficiency when they are either shortened or lengthened over both joints simultaneously. Therefore, the ROM for some of the exercises in this book has been modified to maintain active tension of the targeted muscle.

Another way that muscles limit ROM is related to the fact that muscles become fatigued as they are worked. Muscles typically produce less force on each subsequent repetition, which should result in proportional decreases in ROM. If all other elements of technique (such as alignment, positioning, and stabilization) remain constant, then the range of motion should gradually decrease as the exercise continues. This means that there is no way to prescribe a constant ROM for any resistance exercise, because ROM will always vary as the muscle fatigues.

The study of the concurrent force systems that occur with any joint motion reveals another limit to joint ROM. The pull of a muscle is always a resultant pull of numerous muscle fibers, all in slightly divergent directions. Therefore, while a muscle appears to be contracting in one general direction, it is also applying other forces to the joint. The muscle will always produce a rotational force in one direction to move the bone while also generating a translatory force at the joint in another direction. This translatory force either compresses the joint, distracts the joint, or increases the shear force across the joint as the joint progresses through a full ROM. The ROM for certain exercises in this book has been modified in order to help reduce excessive forces (compressive, distraction, or shearing) on the joint that may lead to long-term joint damage.

Limits to ROM are not always related to the musculoskeletal system, but rather may be due to neurological factors of the control-sensorimotor system. This system includes the mechanisms in which all sensory information is obtained, processed, and transferred back through the spinal cord to the peripheral nervous system. These impulses excite and inhibit the proper concert of muscles in order to produce the desired movement or reaction. The amount of muscle activation the nerves can control varies at different ROMs, particularly when confronted with higher levels of resistance. Simply stated, it is often more difficult to maintain muscle tension on a target muscle when using larger ranges of motion and when using heavier loads.

Optimal Motion

Because people may have different goals in mind, with coinciding options for type and path of motion, and because of the many possible limitations to range of motion, there is no way of determining what "full" range of motion would be for anyone on any exercise without personally assessing that person. However, when all factors are considered, a person can determine an "optimum" range of motion. Optimum range of exercise motion is that amount that best achieves the desired goals and is appropriate for each joint's capabilities under the specific circumstances of the exercise. This means that there would be a different optimum range of motion for each person on each exercise, and that the optimum range would continue to vary on each repetition as the muscles fatigue and as any other variable is altered. A person should never sacrifice any other element of technique in the attempt to increase range of motion.

Alignment

All forces in the universe, apart from God, can be broken down to their core physics and classified into either a pushing force or a pulling force. Alignment is the correct matching of these two basic forces. Muscle physiology demonstrates that a muscle-tendon unit can actively only contract or shorten. This action is classified as a pulling force. Therefore, all muscles can only pull, and none can push. The only way to lengthen a muscle is through the active shortening of the antagonistic muscles or from the application of an outside force. For the purposes of this text, *alignment* is defined as matching the pull of the muscles in opposition to the pull or push of the resistance.

The muscles pull on the bones, which in turn act as a series of levers that can either pull objects toward us, or through the proper combination of pulls, create a pushing force that moves objects away from us. For achieving optimal alignment, you must understand that all pushes the body creates are, in actuality, the combined pull of two or more muscle groups. For example, the positioning of the hands on a barbell chest press affects the alignment of pulling forces. This pressing movement is a pull of the pectorals and deltoids to horizontally adduct the humerus, combined with the pull of the triceps to extend the elbow. Therefore, a person must determine which set of pulls is being targeted in order to position the hands correctly and achieve the proper alignment.

As with any other element of technique, alignment is always dependent on the goals. Keep in mind that since alignment deals with force application, the integrity of the musculoskeletal system should not be compromised for the pursuit of any goal. For instance, on squatting or leg pressing exercises, there are different foot and hip positioning options for aligning the resistance to better target the glutes or the quadriceps. You need to understand the risk to the involved joints that is associated with these different positioning options as well as the potential benefits for the muscles.

To maintain a balance of efficiency and safety, alignment options are usually limited to small adjustments in order to slightly skew force application. This can be done for better targeting of one muscle over another or to simply attempt to get a variation of inter- and intramuscular recruitment patterns. Slight intentional alignment adjustments can be applied that may not seem very efficient for increasing one element of technique, such as ROM, but that better challenge and improve another, such as stabilization.

Positioning

Positioning is another general term often used to convey different meanings. For the purposes of this text, *positioning* is the precise manner in which a person chooses to set the body and place all of its segments before and during any resisted exercise. Positioning is interdependent with the goals involved in selecting the exercise motion itself, and it goes hand in hand with alignment. Maintenance of proper positioning is reliant on stabilization and balance, and it can also be affected by breathing and tempo.

Positioning of the Spine

During any resistance training exercise, a person must consider the positioning of every joint of the body from the ground up, with the most critical segments typically being the pelvis and spine. The spine is the primary component of the axial skeleton and, along with the attached rib cage and pelvis, provides the main support structure of the body. The spine also houses the spinal cord, which is part of the central nervous system and is the key communication line from the brain to the rest of the body, including vital organs and glands.

The unique design and structure of the spinal column not only provides support but also provides for mobility through all three planes of movement. This combined role of providing stability while allowing mobility makes the spine an important consideration in resistance training exercises. It also makes the spine a critical component for the execution of most sport or life movement where both roles are required simultaneously. The exact positioning and movement patterns of the spine that are strengthened during a resistance training program will determine which positions and movements it will perform best during sport and life activities.

Optimal Posture

For all resistance training exercises—other than exercises for targeting the outer trunk musculature and movements designed specifically for improving spinal motion—a person should position the spine in what is called *optimal posture*. When the spine is positioned in optimal posture, it appears to straighten but in fact, barring any structural deviations, maintains certain degrees of its natural curvatures. Optimal posture for resistance training stabilizes the spine with the natural lordotic curvatures in the lumbar and cervical regions in place. Only a slight straightening effect of the thoracic region is noticeable in optimal posture when compared to natural posture. This is in response to the slightly increased retraction of the scapula and associated extension of the thoracic region in order to better stabilize the spine to keep from flexing under load.

Optimal posture provides for optimum structural and functional efficiency of the entire kinetic chain. It promotes optimum length–tension and force-coupling relationships of all the muscles originating from the torso, pelvis, hip, and shoulder girdle. This directly affects the strength and function of all these associated muscles, which, in turn, affects the function and synergistic actions of all other muscles and joint movements of the body. The farther the spine travels in any direction from optimal posture, the less mobility it has in all other directions of movement and the less stable it may become. Figure 3.1 depicts the spine in optimal posture compared to varied positions.

As the spine moves, length–tension relationships between agonists and antagonists change, which further reduces their ability to stabilize or produce force. All spinal movement

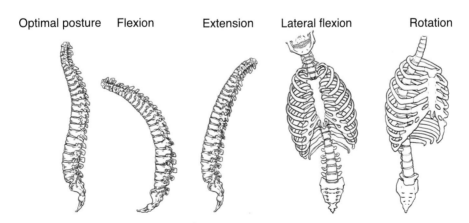

Optimal posture   Flexion   Extension   Lateral flexion   Rotation

Figure 3.1   Optimal posture and spinal movement.

also decreases vertebral space and increases disc compression. But not all movement or disc compression is bad; in fact, vertebral discs rely on compression forces from spinal movement for obtaining nutrients. However, remember that spinal movement, particularly passive movement under load or at high speeds, always results in exponentially increased degrees of compressive forces on the affected discs. This can dramatically increase the level of risk of the exercise and should be evaluated compared to the relative benefits of the exercise in relation to all training goals.

Spinal positioning must also be accompanied by pelvic positioning. Other than sacroiliac joint movement, no pelvic movement is possible without accompanying movement of the spine. An anterior tilt of the pelvis is coupled with lumbar extension, while a posterior pelvic tilt is simply the result of lumbar flexion. Associated hip positioning also accompanies pelvic tilts. This is why a person must also consider the pelvic positioning when determining the positioning of the spine for any exercise. Optimal spinal and pelvic positioning is not only important during resistance exercise but also during many normal life movements. Figures 3.2 and 3.3 compare similar high-risk and reduced-risk positioning options for both resistance exercise and life movements.

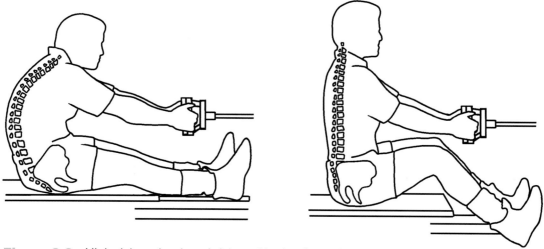

Figure 3.2   High-risk and reduced-risk positioning for resistance training.

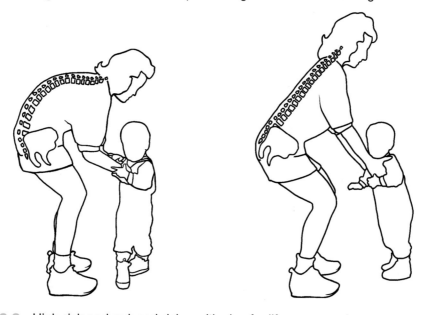

Figure 3.3   High-risk and reduced-risk positioning for life movements.

Positioning Options for Different Goals

At times, changes in positioning options can be made as long as they do not significantly disturb the alignment of forces, are still efficient for performing the desired motion, do not compromise any part of the musculoskeletal system, and can be efficiently stabilized. These optional positioning choices are often used to accomplish different specific goals in a training phase. For example, a lat row can be performed in a variety of positions in order to accomplish different training goals (see figure 3.4).

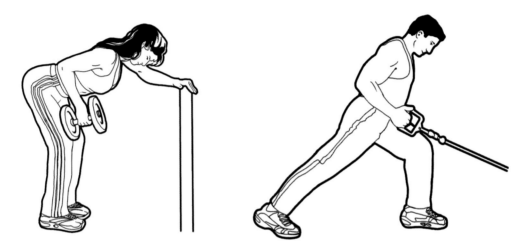

Figure 3.4 Positioning options for accomplishing different goals.

The first positioning option places the body in a symmetrical stance with the arm braced, which provides more support for stabilization. This positioning may be appropriate for a beginner who needs the additional support. It may also be ideal for advanced lifters working with maximal loads during a strength phase of their training cycle.

The second positioning option places the body in a lunge position with no external support. This position will require a much higher demand of the glute and quadriceps of the forward leg for support, and it has a higher stabilization and balance demand. This may be a positioning option selected when attempting to add torque force and a higher stabilization demand on the spine, or it may be used to directly target the posterior oblique subsystem.

Either option may be selected for different people or for the same person during different phases of training to best accomplish specific training goals. The risk-to-benefit ratio could be considered equal if optimal posture, pelvic positioning, and proper alignment are maintained during the exercise movement. Similar comparisons of positioning options can be drawn for any exercise movement or for any muscle group. Try this yourself by simply observing the subtle yet important differences in the alignment and positioning options that are pictured and described for each of the different exercises for any muscle group in this book.

Stabilization

For the purposes of this book, *stabilization* may be defined as the internal ability to control all desired movement or nonmovement of the body and its segments in response to the environment and changes in center of gravity. Stabilization of any joint may be classified as a *static demand* or a *dynamic demand*. All exercises require combinations of both and also have some level of *balance demand*.

Static stability is characterized by the ability to hold a set joint position against resistance through isometric muscle action. The ability to maintain optimal posture of the spine and proper positioning of the pelvis during a squat movement is an example of static stabilization.

Dynamic stability is characterized by the type of stability a joint must exhibit while in motion in order to control the range and the path of motion in the selected plane. For example, the hip must be allowed to flex and made to extend against resistance during the squat movement. However, the hips must also be dynamically stabilized to keep from adducting or internally rotating during the movement in order to prevent the knees from angling in and placing undue stress on the joints and connective tissue. Dynamic stability is also necessary to stabilize joints upon impact, such as the ankle and hip when running. This type of dynamic stability can be referred to as *impact stability*.

Balance Demands

Balance is definitely an intricate part of stability. Balance is defined as the process of maintaining one's center of gravity within the body's base of support. Balance relies predominantly on the activation of specialized reflex actions that vary from small shifting responses of the ankle or hip to stepping strategies and associated upper extremity movement to regain center of gravity. Reflex actions can be divided into two general types: body-righting reflexes and tilting-response reflexes. Certain life or exercise movements may require combinations of both types of reflex actions, but in most movements, one reflex type dominates over the other.

• *Body-righting reflexes* tend to dominate when standing on or moving across a stable surface or platform. Most life and sport movements will typically be dominated by this type of reflex action because people typically live and play on stable surfaces. Body-righting reflexes are included in training whenever a person's base of support is reduced, such as a gymnast performing her routine on a balance beam, or whenever an exercise is performed on one foot, such as the dumbbell single-leg hip extension (demonstrated in figure 3.5).

Figure 3.5 Body-righting reflex training.

• *Tilting-response reflexes* are dominant when the supportive surface a person is standing on or moving across is also able to move beneath the person or is unstable. These types of balance demands are less common but can occur at times, such as when hiking across a steep, rocky terrain or riding a skateboard. Similar tilting-response reflex demands are trained when exercising on unstable devices such as balance boards, instability disks, or Swiss balls. Since the demand for this type of reflex action is less common in life, the number of exercises in this book that focus on training tilting-response reflexes is also limited. (One such exercise is the balance board squat pictured in figure 3.6.)

Figure 3.6 Tilting-response reflex training.

The Stabilization Process

Without stabilization, other elements of technique—particularly the positioning, the alignment, and the motion—would all be compromised. Stabilization requires the integrated function of all three systems involved in human movement. The passive-skeletal system relies on the active-muscular system for holding joint position. The active system in turn is reliant on its interdependent relationship with the control-sensorimotor system for reflex actions and commands to control and coordinate the proper activations of the combination of muscles needed to provide stability.

The control system provides for *kinesthesia,* which is the conscious awareness of joint position and joint movement. Kinesthesia is imperative for stabilization and balance, and it results from processing input information to the central nervous system from visual, vestibular, and proprioceptive sources. Proprioception is the cumulative neural input from all the numerous afferent receptors in the muscles, joints, connective tissues, and even in the skin. This information is then processed at the appropriate level, and commands are sent to the active system to make the needed adjustments to stabilize the passive system.

Improved neuromuscular efficiency is needed for improved stabilization and balance. Since improving neuromuscular efficiency is a process, so then is stabilization. In time, *motor programs* that combine movements and stabilization strategies can be performed with little or no conscious thought and concurrently will require a lower level of motor control. Once an exercise has been performed enough times, the stabilization and balance demands are met with little or no conscious effort.

Once an exercise is mastered or performed efficiently with an automated level of control, the exercise challenge can be progressed in many different ways. Increases in intensity or volume are the most common ways to progress an exercise challenge, but you can also consider raising the stability and balance demands as an alternative. Reducing the base of support by removing one foot from the ground, or reducing the visual sensory input by simply closing your eyes during the movement, are also options for progression toward accomplishing different goals.

Stabilization and the Core

Stabilization begins with the spine and is first initiated by the local spinal stabilization subsystem known as the inner unit, or core. Research confirms that in healthy individuals, activation of the core muscles occurs before any movement of the body or a body segment. This confirms that the core muscles are essential for optimal stabilization and are stimulated any time stability and balance are challenged. This does not mean, however, that simply performing exercises while standing on unstable apparatus (such as balance boards and instability disks) is the best way to develop optimal core function.

Stabilization and core muscle involvement are specific to the environment and to the conditions in which they are trained. Therefore, attempting to train the core muscles by triggering tilting-response reflexes may not transfer to core activation for life's predominant needs. As discussed in chapter 2, the core muscles also assist with respiratory function, and this should also be considered. If proper breathing methods are integrated into any exercise movement, they should help to activate the core muscles more efficiently for performing their stabilization actions synergistically. Therefore, optimal training of the core muscles is not totally dependent on the exercise selection but is dependent on the exercise techniques as well.

Tempo

Probably the most overlooked element of exercise technique is tempo. *Tempo* is defined as the specific movement speed of the body or segments during any given exercise. Tempo for resistance training deals with the actual speed of each repetition and has great potential for bringing about different training adaptations. The neuromuscular system not only adapts to the type, range, and specificity of motion but to the speed of motion as well. Tempo has traditionally been taught in a nonspecific, very general manner or occasionally been presented as part of a training philosophy that promotes only one tempo as optimal regardless of the goal. Simple review of the facts concerning the basic physiology of muscle adaptation to different speeds of contraction and different amounts of time under tension demonstrates that there is no one tempo that could possibly be the best for accomplishing every training goal.

The Science of Tempo

Mechanoreceptors within the joints, connective tissue, and the muscles themselves monitor not only the type, range, and specificity of motion but also the speed of motion. For some training goals, the total amount of muscle force is not as important as the rate of muscle force production. Therefore, there will be specific tempos to use for targeting specific types of strength gains. For example, slower tempos with pauses at the eccentric-isometric phase (when the primary muscles are lengthened) would be better for targeting maximal strength and isometric strength gains. Conversely, faster tempos with no pauses at the eccentric-isometric phase that induce a stretch reflex would be more appropriate for training explosive strength and increasing one's power.

Biomechanical factors are also associated with tempo and should be considered in order to better match every exercise to each person's anatomical makeup and individual abilities. For people with longer limb lengths, the joints and the weight loads applied will be moving at faster rates when exercising at the same tempo as individuals with shorter limbs. This is simply due to the larger ranges of proportional joint motion incurred by longer-limbed people to produce the same general movement as their shorter counterparts. Therefore, slower tempos may be appropriate for these people to accomplish similar training goals.

Tempo Assignment

Numerical representations for desired repetition speed or tempo are nothing new. Arthur Jones long ago advised a specific two-digit tempo for use with his Nautilus line of equipment. The first number expressed the eccentric or lowering phase of the exercise, while the second number represented the concentric or lifting phase of the repetition. Poliquin, who has probably placed more importance on tempo than any other expert to my knowledge, has promoted a system developed by Ian King that uses a three-digit number to express tempo. The addition of the third number denotes an isometric phase of the repetition that would exist at some level between the eccentric and concentric phases. This led me to develop a four-number system for tempo that also recognizes another isometric phase that would occur during the end of the concentric phase and the beginning of the subsequent eccentric phase.

This four-digit number method to express tempo is used in the program design in chapter 9. The first number represents the eccentric phase of the exercise, which is typically when the weight is lowered. The next number represents the eccentric-isometric phase and is the conversion point of eccentric and concentric muscle action. The assignment of this number is often the key for achieving different strength adaptations and accomplishing different training goals. The third number represents the concentric phase of the repetition, which is typically when the weight is being lifted. The fourth number represents the concentric-isometric phase and is often considered as somewhat of a resting point for many pushing exercises.

No specific tempos are given in the instructions for the exercises presented in this book. This is again to stress that several different tempos could be used for any exercise in order to target different training goals. The speed of motion described by the instructions accompanying each exercise is a slow, controlled movement speed with momentary pauses at the starting and ending points of each exercise. This description would imply about a one-second eccentric-isometric phase and concentric-isometric phase. This tempo is conducive for learning to master the movement pattern, stabilize the instructed alignment and positioning, and integrate the breathing technique. However, once the exercise movement is mastered and the breathing method is synchronized, changes in tempo are suggested to better match training goals and training phases.

Breathing

Breathing is another element of technique that has often been oversimplified or completely overlooked. Of course, most books and instructors recommend breathing, but there is rarely any technically sound method or any scientific rationale associated with the advice. Breathing is a vital mechanical function requiring the integrated and coordinated action of several muscle groups, whether a person is consciously aware of this or not. Chapter 2 (in the section on the inner unit) details the sequence of muscle actions involved in the breathing cycle. You may want to turn back for a quick review before continuing, because the following recommended breathing methods are based on this information regarding the body's designed respiratory process.

The inner unit, or core, has dual roles that it must perform simultaneously. The core is required to assist with respiration while also providing spinal and pelvic stabilization. These seemingly different responsibilities of the core are actually logical, harmonious functions of its design. With the proper breathing method, the mechanics and associated muscle actions of respiration will actually assist with control of intra-abdominal pressure and provide for increased stabilization of the spine and pelvic girdle.

For most exercises, inhalation will begin as the movement begins, which is often the eccentric phase of the movement. Inhalation should be initiated with the uninhibited contraction of the diaphragm. This creates a downward pressure on the viscera in the abdominal cavity while simultaneously helping the lungs to draw in more air. The downward pressure forces the contents of the abdominal cavity down, back, and forward causing a slight distension and tightening of the abdominal wall. This results in increased intra-abdominal pressure and combines with associated neurological reactions of the other core muscles to create joint stiffness of the spine and increase stabilization of the pelvis and sacroiliac joints.

As inhalation continues, there should be an expansion and slight elevation of the rib cage, which allows for maximal lung volume and also further straightens the spine and helps to stabilize optimal posture. However, inhalation should not produce any significant elevation of the scapula or shrugging of the shoulders, because these muscle actions will increase stress to the structures of the cervical spine. During the eccentric-isometric phase, the breath can be held momentarily and the abdominal muscles can be isometrically contracted to produce a momentary Valsalva maneuver and provide maximal spinal stability.

Exhalation begins as the movement is reversed, which is typically during the concentric phase. To assist with maintenance of optimal posture and avoid the tendency to flex the spine upon exhalation, the person should activate a contraction of the transverse abdominis and draw the abdominal wall in slightly toward the spine. This helps to maintain higher levels of intra-abdominal and intrathoracic pressure, and again is linked to co-contractions of other core muscles that will assist in stabilizing the spine and pelvis. You should also note that full exhalation during most resistance exercises is not recommended. Maintenance of some air in the lungs helps maintain intrathoracic pressure and keep the rib cage partially expanded and elevated, which helps to continue stabilization of optimal posture.

At the concentric-isometric phase, a tight contraction of the transverse abdominis (just short of concaving the abdominal wall) along with an isometric contraction of the outer abdominal and trunk muscles can often be felt. As inhalation and the eccentric movement begins, the person should again initiate a contraction of the diaphragm and somewhat relax the transverse abdominis to allow for the slight distension of the abdominal wall to repeat the inhalation process.

For a few exercises, inhalation will begin with the concentric phase, and the entire process will be reversed from what has just been described. This is because of the inverse maximal stability demands for the particular movement. These breathing methods will take time to master and integrate into every exercise. You should first try them with the core activation exercises presented in this book and use slower tempos for all exercises in the beginning in order to best develop these breathing methods. In time and with consistent use, this method will become a natural reaction of neuromuscular control and may increase the overall effectiveness and safety of your training.

Relationships of Technique Elements

As stated, all elements of technique are interdependent and have what can even be considered co-dependent relationships. All elements of technique should be directly related to and affected by the identified training goals associated with any specific exercise. Only then can the movement itself—along with the alignment, positioning, and stabilization options—be selected. Even the tempo, and to a lesser degree the specific breathing method, is reliant on the identified training goal. A change in any element of technique will in turn affect the others. For example, if the positioning option is changed, then the movement is altered and the alignment of forces is also automatically changed. Stabilization strategies will need to be modified, as will tempo and perhaps breathing. A similar case can be made for altering any element of technique, because they all must be coordinated to provide for the optimal training stimuli that best achieve the training goal and also decrease associated risk. Therefore, it is important to consider all elements of technique collectively (as opposed to independently) and to realize the overall benefits or risks associated with any modifications.

Core and Trunk Exercises

This chapter presents several exercises that target and strengthen the core and trunk muscles. Core control and activation, along with the integration of the suggested breathing method, are particularly important elements of technique for these exercises. The exercise selections can be classified in two general categories—those that develop the ability to stabilize the spine and pelvis, and those that develop the ability to move the spine. Spinal structure and function, as well as specific muscle physiology and all biomechanical factors, were considered when developing the instructions for all elements of technique, such as alignment, positioning, motion, stabilization, and suggested breathing method.

These exercise selections vary in their difficulty of stabilization or movement demands in order to provide a well-balanced collection of movements to challenge individuals of all strength and fitness levels. Variations and modifications that increase or decrease the level of challenge are also provided within the description section for many exercises. These additional suggestions combined with the information provided in the first three chapters will assist you in selecting the core and trunk exercises that best address your own performance and aesthetic goals. In addition to the abundant information on efficient exercise selection provided throughout this book, chapter 9 covers program design and will help you combine exercise selections into effective resistance training routines as well as assist you in designing long-term exercise programs. Remember to incorporate the elements of technique discussed in chapter 3 and summarized below. Consider them as steps or guidelines when selecting any of the exercises in this book (or from any other source).

1. Define the goal.
2. Select the movement pattern.
3. Consider alignment and positioning options.
4. Focus on stabilization over movement.
5. Plan and control the tempo.
6. Integrate breathing control.
7. Perform a specific warm-up set for each exercise.

Four-Point Core Activation

The Four-Point Core Activation is a beginning spinal stabilization exercise. This exercise is designed to provide the most neurologically advantageous position to learn core activation and develop strength and control of the transverse abdominis. The direct gravitational pull on the viscera provides for the best proprioception for activation of the core muscles and provides an internal resistance for the transverse abdominis to work against. This exercise can be progressed by elevating an arm or leg to move to a three-point position; it can then be further progressed by adding actual movement of the limb, while coordinating tempo with the breathing method.

Target Muscles

Core (transverse abdominis, diaphragm, pelvic floor muscles, and transversospinalis group)

Joint Motions

None

Four-Point Core Activation

Alignment and Positioning

1. Assume a position on the hands and knees, with the knees placed directly below the hips, the hands directly below the shoulders, and the elbows slightly bent.

2. Position the spine in optimal posture, and hold the head in a neutral position with the eyes looking straight down.

Motion and Stabilization

1. Begin to inhale and allow the abdominal area to distend without losing the posture position of the spine.

2. Slowly breathe out and contract the transverse abdominis by pulling the belly button up toward the spine. Focus on stabilizing the spine and pelvis.

3. Exhale all remaining air while continuing to tighten the abdominal wall and stabilize the spine. Slowly begin to inhale and repeat.

Quadraplex

The Quadraplex can also be considered a "two-point core activation" exercise with added movement of the arm and contralateral leg. The required muscle actions of the shoulder and hip to move and decelerate the limbs, along with the increased demand on the trunk and core muscles for stabilization, make this exercise an advanced progression in core training. Keep in mind that the focus should be placed on stabilization of the spine and pelvis and on the core activation as opposed to the limb movements. To decrease the challenge of the exercise, simply hold the arm and leg in the up position rather than raising and lowering them.

Target Muscles

Core (transverse abdominis, diaphragm, pelvic floor muscles, and transversospinalis group), contralateral hip extensors and shoulder flexors, contralateral hip abductors and scapular stabilizers

Joint Motions

Shoulder flexion and hip extension

Alignment and Positioning

1. Start on the hands and knees with one knee placed directly below the hip and the opposite hand directly below the shoulder. Place the opposite leg and arm straight out from the body and just off the ground.

2. Slowly draw a deep breath and allow the abdominal area to distend while maintaining posture in the spine and keeping the head in a neutral position.

Motion and Stabilization

1. Slowly begin to exhale, and draw the belly button to the spine while raising the arm and opposite leg without losing optimal posture of the spine or positioning of the pelvis.

2. Hold the top position while continuing to contract the transverse abdominis and stabilizing the spine in optimal posture.

3. Slowly begin to inhale, allowing the abdominal area to distend and the leg and arm to lower while maintaining posture.

Bent-Leg Raises

This exercise trains core activation in a supine position. The added action of the hip flexor muscles, combined with the inertia of the moving leg, make this exercise substantially more demanding on the core and trunk muscles for stabilization of the spine while still encouraging proper respiratory functions. As with any supine exercise, the upward distension of the viscera is directly resisted by gravity, presenting a greater challenge for diaphragmatic action. This exercise can be progressed by increasing the incline position of the body, straighten-

ing the leg, or using faster tempos and leg movement. This exercise may also be performed on a Swiss ball for an increased stabilization challenge.

Target Muscles

Core (transverse abdominis, diaphragm, pelvic floor muscles, and transversospinalis group), spinal flexors, hip flexors

Joint Motions

Hip flexion

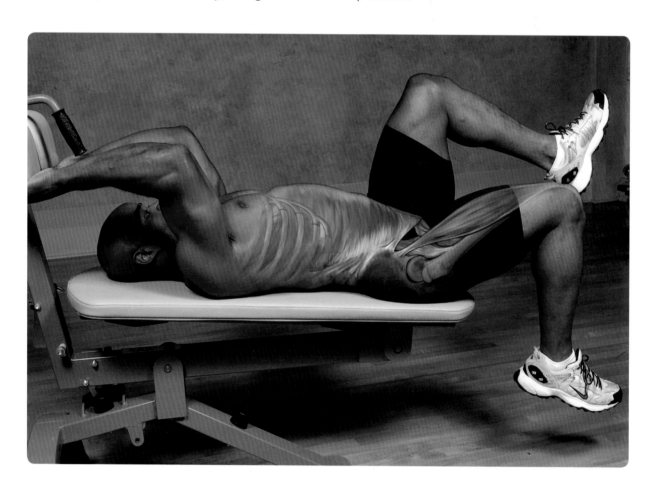

Alignment and Positioning

1. Lie supine while in good posture, with a natural arch in the lower spine and the knees bent and held directly above the hips.

Motion and Stabilization

1. Draw a deep breath, causing the abdominal area to slightly distend upward, with the spine held firm in posture. Slowly lower one leg, keeping the knee in a bent position.

2. Hold, then slowly begin to exhale and draw the belly button toward the spine while raising the leg back up to the starting position and maintaining the natural arch in the lower spine.

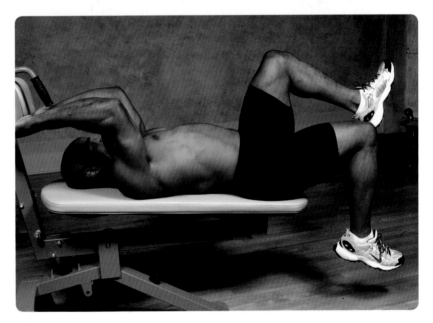

Incline Bench Trunk Flexion

This exercise targets the abdominal and oblique musculature and trains flexion of the spine in a gravity-assisted position. The incline angle and stable bench allow the lifter to more easily achieve his or her maximal amount of spinal flexion. Variations in the amount of incline can be used to increase or decrease resistance as desired. Depending on the lifter's ability and goals, altering leg position to increase or decrease hip flexor involvement is also a viable option.

Target Muscles

Spinal flexors (rectus abdominis, obliques)

Joint Motions

Trunk flexion

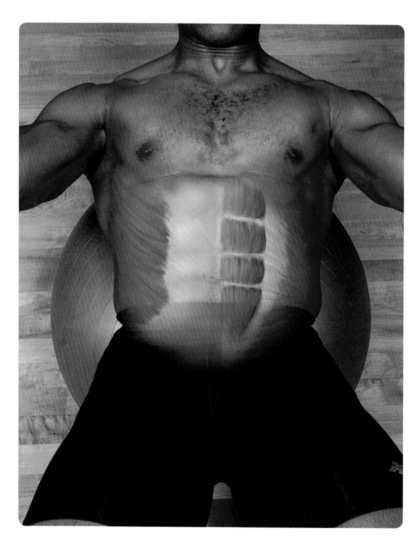

Alignment and Positioning

1. Lie supine on the inclined bench, with the feet braced lightly on the anchor pad or wall, and with the hips and knees bent about 60 and 90 degrees respectively.

2. Spread the legs so the feet are angled out about 45 degrees (or at about 2 and 10 o'clock).

3. Place the fists under the chin and begin with a full breath of air, the shoulders just off the bench, and tension on the abdominal muscles.

Motion and Stabilization

1. Slowly begin to exhale and pull the ribs toward the pelvis, attempting to move one vertebra at a time.

2. Hold the top position while continuing to exhale, contracting the abdominal muscles, and stabilizing the neck.

3. Slowly begin to inhale, and lower the torso back down to the starting position while stabilizing the head position and maintaining tension on the abdominal muscles.

Swiss Ball Trunk Flexion

The shape and yielding surface of the Swiss ball allow for a greater degree of motion because the spine can begin in a position of extension. This exercise targets the abdominal and oblique musculature to flex the spine; it requires greater core and trunk muscle demand as compared to performing this movement on a bench and therefore presents moderate balance challenges. Different angles of resistance can be applied by simply repositioning the body on the ball. Shifting the body down on the ball creates more of an incline angle and decreases resistance. Shifting more of the lower back and pelvis onto the ball flattens out the angle of pull and increases the resistance.

Target Muscles

Spinal flexors (rectus abdominis, obliques)

Joint Motions

Trunk flexion

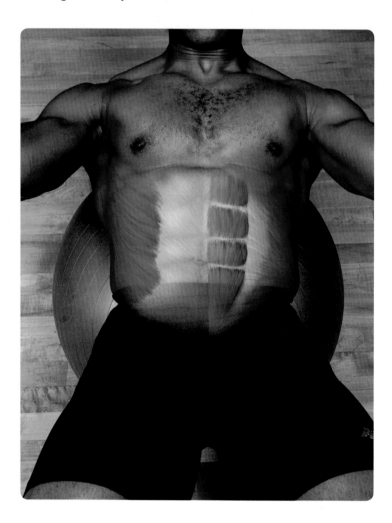

Alignment and Positioning

1. Lie supine on the ball with the feet spread and placed on the floor.

2. Adjust the desired angle on the ball, and let the spine bend back over the ball as available and comfortable for the spine.

3. Place the fists just under the chin, and begin with a full breath of air and with tension on the abdominal muscles.

Motion and Stabilization

1. Slowly begin to exhale, and pull the ribs toward the pelvis, attempting to move one vertebra at a time.

2. Hold the top position while continuing to exhale, contracting the abdominal muscles, and relaxing the neck.

3. Slowly begin to inhale, and lower the torso back down to the starting position while maintaining the head position and keeping tension on the abdominal muscles.

Flat Bench Reverse Trunk Flexion

This exercise targets the abdominal and oblique musculature and trains flexion of the spine in a reverse movement. The reverse trunk flexion contracts the abdominal muscles in an insertion-to-origin pattern opposite that of trunk flexion exercises. This movement also targets flexion of the lumbar region of the spine rather than the flexion of the thoracic region produced from a typical trunk flexion exercise. Different angles of incline or decline can be used with an adjustable bench to increase or decrease resistance.

Target Muscles

Spinal flexors (rectus abdominis, obliques)

Joint Motions

Trunk flexion (lumbar region)

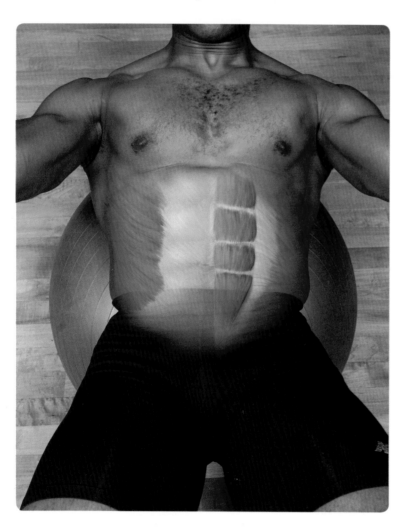

Flat Bench Reverse Trunk Flexion

Alignment and Positioning

1. Lie supine on the bench with the hips and knees bent about 90 degrees.

2. Anchor the body with the arms, and begin with the head just off the pad to target the neck flexors as well as the trunk flexors.

3. Posteriorly tilt the pelvis to flatten the lower back. Begin with a full breath of air and with tension on the abdominal muscles.

Motion and Stabilization

1. Slowly begin to exhale and pull the pelvis toward the ribs, attempting to move one vertebra at a time.

2. Hold the top position while continuing to exhale, contracting the abdominal muscles, and stabilizing the head in a slightly flexed position.

3. Slowly begin to inhale while lowering the pelvis back down to the starting position and maintaining tension on the abdominal muscles. *Note:* The head can rest on the bench if the neck flexors become fatigued.

Swiss Ball Reverse Trunk Flexion

This exercise targets the abdominal and oblique musculature and trains flexion of the spine in a reverse movement. Contracting the abdominal muscles in an insertion-to-origin pattern may develop an initial, and possibly increased, activation of the lower fibers of the rectus abdominis. Use of the ball requires additional core and trunk muscle recruitment to correct for balance challenges, and it increases the range of motion by allowing the spine to begin in a position of extension. Increased resistance can be applied by simply repositioning the body on the ball. Shifting the body down on the ball creates more of an incline angle and increases resistance, while shifting more of the lower back and pelvis onto the ball decreases resistance.

Target Muscles

Spinal flexors (rectus abdominis, obliques)

Joint Motions

Trunk flexion (lumbar region)

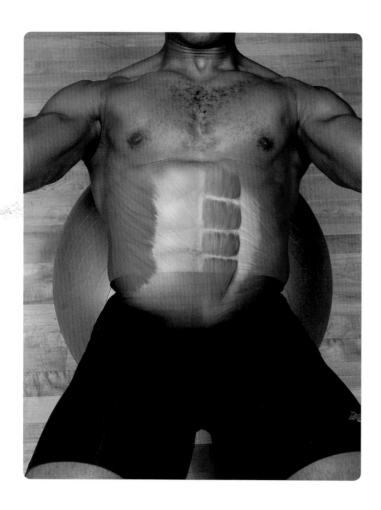

Alignment and Positioning

1. Lie supine on the ball with the hips and knees bent about 90 degrees.

2. Anchor the body with the arms, and begin with the spine pressed against and extended over the ball as available and comfortable for the spine.

3. Begin with a full breath of air, the head held in a neutral position, and tension on the abdominal muscles.

Motion and Stabilization

1. Slowly begin to exhale and pull the pelvis toward the ribs, attempting to move one vertebra at a time.

2. Hold the top position while continuing to exhale, contracting the abdominal muscles, and stabilizing the head in a slightly flexed position.

3. Slowly begin to inhale, and lower the pelvis back down to the starting position while maintaining tension on the abdominal muscles.

Incline Bench Trunk Extension

This exercise targets the spinal extensors, particularly those of the thoracic region, with some hip extensor assistance. Using a stable bench allows the lifter to more specifically control the degree and region of spinal movement. It is often difficult for some individuals to produce extension of the mid and upper back without hyperextending the lower back. Variations in the amount of incline can be used to increase or decrease resistance as desired. Altering leg position to increase or decrease hip extensor involvement is also a viable option.

Target Muscles

Spinal erectors (iliocostalis, longissimus, spinalis), transversospinalis group

Joint Motions

Trunk extension (thoracic region)

Incline Bench Trunk Extension

Alignment and Positioning

1. Lie prone on the inclined bench with the legs spread comfortably and the feet braced against the floor.

2. Place the arms against the body, out to the side, or overhead depending on the desired resistance and your level of strength. Begin with a full breath of air, the chest just off the bench, and with tension on the extensors.

Motion and Stabilization

1. Slowly begin to exhale. Activate the core to pull the abdomen slightly off the bench while pulling the shoulder blades back and together.

2. Continue to exhale and attempt to extend the thoracic spine one vertebra at a time without hyperextending the lower back. Then hold the top position and further contract the core.

3. Slowly begin to inhale, and lower the torso back down to the starting position while maintaining the head position and keeping tension on the extensors.

Swiss Ball Trunk Extension

This exercise targets the spinal extensors, particularly those in the thoracic region, with some hip extensor assistance. Using a ball and beginning in a position of spinal flexion can increase the range of motion. The ball also requires some different core, trunk, and hip musculature recruitment to correct for tilting-response challenges. Variations in the angle and weight load can be made by adjusting the body position on the ball. Depending on the lifter's ability and goals, altering leg positions to increase or decrease hip extensor involvement is also a viable option.

Target Muscles

Spinal erectors (iliocostalis, longissimus, spinalis), transversospinalis group

Joint Motions

Trunk extension (thoracic region)

Alignment and Positioning

1. Lie prone on the ball with the legs spread comfortably and the feet braced against the floor.

2. Bend the spine comfortably over the ball, and place the arms against the body, out to the side, or overhead depending on the desired resistance.

3. Begin with a full breath of air, the chest just off the ball, and with tension on the extensors.

Motion and Stabilization

1. Slowly begin to exhale, activate the core, and pull the shoulder blades together and back.

2. Begin to extend the thoracic spine, attempting to move one thoracic vertebra at a time and being careful not to hyperextend the lower back.

3. Hold the top position. Then slowly begin to inhale while lowering the torso back down to the starting position, maintaining the head position and keeping tension on the extensors.

Half Ball Trunk Lateral Flexion

This exercise isolaterally targets the quadratus lumborum, internal obliques, and portions of the external obliques, rectus abdominis, and spinal extensors to the side of movement. Use of the ball can increase the range of motion if beginning in a position of lateral flexion to the opposite side, and it also requires some different core, trunk, and hip musculature recruitment to correct for tilting-response challenges. Variations in the angle and weight load can be made by adjusting the body position on the ball. Depending on the lifter's ability and goals, altering leg position to increase or decrease hip abductor involvement is also a viable option.

Target Muscles

Spinal lateral flexors, quadratus lumborum, internal obliques, ipsilateral spinal flexors, ipsilateral trunk extensors

Joint Motions

Trunk lateral flexion

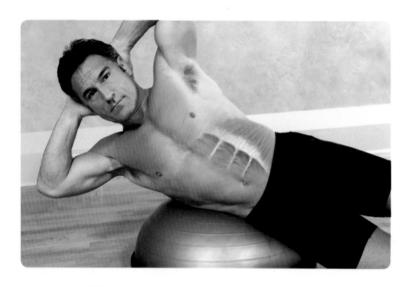

Alignment and Positioning

1. Lie on your side over the half ball, with the bottom leg placed in front of the body and the top leg straight and slightly behind the body.

2. Bend the spine comfortably over the ball, place the bottom arm overhead, and place the top arm against the body or overhead depending on the desired resistance. Begin with a full breath of air.

Motion and Stabilization

1. Slowly begin to exhale, activate the core, and pull the lower ribs toward the crest of the pelvic girdle, attempting to move laterally, one vertebra at a time.

2. Pull the trunk up and over as far as possible without flexing or extending the spine, while continuing to exhale.

3. Hold, then slowly begin to inhale while lowering the torso back down to the starting position, maintaining the head position and keeping tension on the lateral flexors.

Supine Trunk Rotation

This exercise is designed to begin working on loaded isolated rotation of the spine. It allows the lifter to begin strengthening the external obliques and associated trunk rotators in a stabilized position. Develop the strength and control of these muscles before progressing to more integrated movements. Once integrated movements are required, the body will use other joints and muscles to compensate for any weakness or lack of movement in spinal rotation.

Target Muscles

Spinal rotators (external oblique, contralateral internal oblique), spinal flexors, transversospinalis group

Joint Motions

Trunk rotation

Alignment and Positioning

1. Lie supine on the floor with the feet braced lightly on a low bench or chair.

2. Place one leg over the other. Rotate the pelvis and legs over about 35 to 45 degrees with the sternum still facing up.

3. Place the bottom hand on the side and the other hand behind the head. Begin with the shoulders slightly off the ground and a full breath of air.

Motion and Stabilization

1. Slowly begin to exhale, activate the core, and pull the rib cage slightly up and over to align with the pelvis, keeping the head in a neutral position.

2. Hold the top position while continuing to exhale and contracting the core, abdominal, and oblique muscles.

3. Slowly begin to inhale while lowering the torso back down and over to the starting position, maintaining the head position and keeping tension on the abdominal muscles and obliques.

Machine Trunk Rotation

This exercise is designed to strengthen isolated spinal rotation and the anterior oblique subsystem. The use of the machine allows the lifter to develop rotational movement with little stabilization demand, and it provides a brace to anchor the opposite thigh and avoid promoting high levels of hip adductor assistance. This beginning rotational exercise helps to assess and strengthen present active ranges of available spinal rotation before performing more advanced rotational exercises.

Target Muscles

Anterior oblique subsystem (external oblique, contralateral hip adductors, contralateral internal oblique), rectus abdominis, transversospinalis group

Joint Motions

Trunk rotation

Alignment and Positioning

1. Position the machine to about 45 degrees or the specific amount of spinal rotation desired. Be sure not to set the limit any farther than you can presently actively rotate the spine without resistance!

2. Begin in a rotated position but with good posture and with close to a natural arch in the lower back. Position the arms over the pads and the legs firmly against the pads.

3. Draw a deep breath, allowing the abdominal area to slightly distend with the spine. Avoid any shrugging of the shoulder blades.

Motion and Stabilization

1. Slowly begin to exhale, activate the core, and begin rotating the torso while avoiding flexing or extending the spine.

2. Rotate just slightly past a neutral position (where the torso and pelvis would be directly aligned) while continuing to exhale and contracting the core muscles.

3. Slowly begin to inhale while rotating back to the starting position, allowing the abdominal muscles to slightly distend and keeping the scapula stabilized.

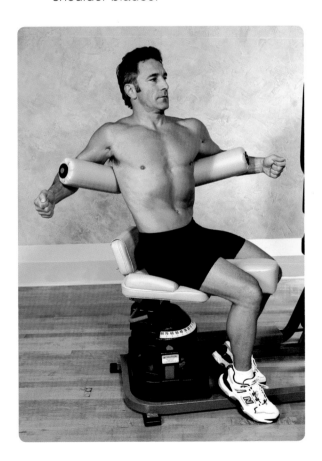
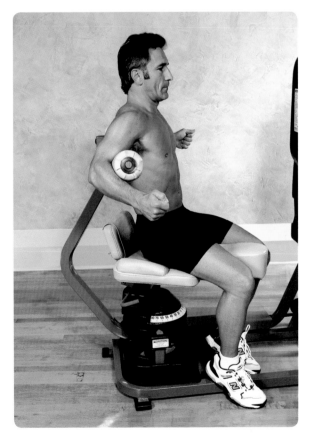

Cable Trunk Rotation With Flexion

This exercise is designed to begin teaching resisted integrated trunk flexion and rotation of the spine. It targets and strengthens the external obliques and associated trunk rotators and flexors while the person is in a standing position that requires lower body musculature for stabilization. This movement pattern would be somewhat transferable to the spinal action involved when throwing a baseball, javelin, or any other object (or even a punch). Teaching and strengthening the body to produce forces in this way should precede faster, more ballistic exercises involving spinal rotation.

Target Muscles

Anterior oblique subsystem (external oblique, contralateral hip adductors, contralateral internal oblique), rectus abdominis, transversospinalis group

Joint Motions

Trunk rotation

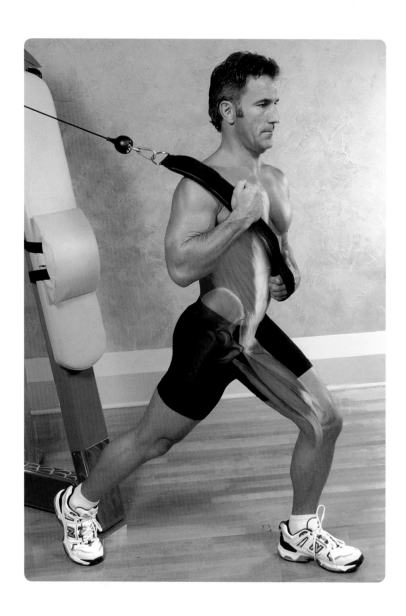

Cable Trunk Rotation With Flexion

Alignment and Positioning

1. Stand in a lunge position, with the back leg straight. Lean the trunk forward, placing the weight over the lead leg while maintaining good posture.

2. Place the strap diagonally over the shoulder and torso opposite to the lead leg.

3. Draw a deep breath, and begin with the trunk in good posture and the pelvis and head squarely aligned.

Motion and Stabilization

1. Slowly begin to exhale. Activate the core while simultaneously flexing and gradually rotating the spine, keeping the pelvis and lower body stabilized.

2. Flex and rotate the spine as far as possible while continuing to exhale and contracting the core muscles.

3. Hold, then slowly begin to inhale while slowly extending and rotating the spine back up to the starting position, maintaining pelvic and leg positioning.

Cable Trunk Rotation With Pull

This exercise is designed to teach integrated and loaded rotation of the spine. It targets and strengthens the external obliques and associated trunk rotators while the person is in a standing position. It also integrates lower body musculature for stabilization and posterior upper body muscles for the pulling movement. Teach the body how to deal with forces in this manner before progressing to faster, more ballistic exercises involving spinal rotation.

Target Muscles

Posterior oblique subsystem (latissimus dorsi, contralateral gluteus maximus, hip external rotators), spinal rotators (external oblique, contralateral internal oblique, transversospinalis group), shoulder and scapular pulling muscles

Joint Motions

Trunk rotation, scapular retraction, shoulder horizontal abduction, elbow flexion

Cable Trunk Rotation With Pull

Alignment and Positioning

1. Stand in a lunge position, with the back leg straight. Lean the trunk forward, placing the weight over the lead leg while maintaining good posture.

2. Grasp the handle with the hand opposite of the lead leg, and begin with the arm straight and perpendicular to the trunk, with the elbow out.

3. Draw a deep breath, and begin with the trunk rotated, keeping the pelvis and head squarely aligned.

Motion and Stabilization

1. Slowly begin to exhale, activate the core, and rotate the spine while pulling the arm out and back, keeping the head and pelvis straight.

2. Rotate the spine and pull the arm back while continuing to exhale and contracting the core muscles.

3. Hold, then slowly begin to inhale while rotating the torso back around and down to the starting position, maintaining the head and pelvic position.

Cable Trunk Rotation With Press

This exercise also teaches you how to perform integrated and loaded rotation of the spine. It targets and strengthens the external obliques and associated trunk rotators from a standing position. It also integrates lower body musculature for stabilization and anterior upper body muscles for the pulling movement. Teach the body how to deal with forces in this manner before progressing to faster, more ballistic exercises involving spinal rotation.

Target Muscles

Anterior oblique subsystem (external oblique, contralateral hip adductors, contralateral internal oblique), rectus abdominis, transversospinalis group, shoulder and scapular pushing muscles

Joint Motions

Trunk rotation, scapular protraction, shoulder horizontal adduction, elbow extension

Alignment and Positioning

1. Grasp the upper pulley handle and step forward with the opposite leg into a lunge position, with the back leg straight and the trunk leaned forward while maintaining good posture.

2. Position the arm up and aligned perpendicularly to the trunk, with the elbow out.

3. Begin with the spine rotated and the feet, pelvis, and head squarely aligned. Draw a deep breath.

Motion and Stabilization

1. Slowly begin to exhale while rotating the trunk and pressing the handle down and around. Keep the elbow pointed out and keep the head and pelvis straight.

2. Continue to rotate the spine and press the hand down while continuing to exhale and contracting the core muscles.

3. Hold, then slowly begin to inhale while rotating the torso back around and up to the starting position, maintaining the head and pelvic position.

Compound Lower Body Exercises

In this chapter, several exercises that target and strengthen the pelvic, hip, and leg muscles of the lower body are presented. Integration of core and trunk muscle stabilization is an essential element of technique for these exercises. Exercise selections for the lower body can be classified in two general categories—compound exercises (such as squats, lunges, and presses) and isolated exercises for the ankles, knees, and hips. This chapter presents compound leg movements that can also be classified as varied general movement patterns. Lower body and spinal structure and function, along with specific muscle physiology and biomechanical factors, were considered when developing the instructions for all elements of technique, such as alignment, positioning, motion, stabilization, and suggested breathing method.

These exercise selections vary in their difficulty of stabilization or movement demands in order to provide a well-balanced collection of movements to challenge individuals of all strength and fitness levels. Variations and modifications that will increase or decrease the level of challenge are also provided in the description section for many exercises. These additional suggestions combined with the information provided in the first three chapters should assist you in selecting the lower body exercises that best address your own performance and aesthetic goals. In addition to the abundant information on efficient exercise selection provided throughout this book, chapter 9 covers program design and will help you combine exercise selections into effective resistance training routines as well as assist you in designing long-term exercise programs. Remember to incorporate the elements of technique discussed in chapter 3 and summarized below. Consider them as steps or guidelines when selecting any of the exercises in this book (or from any other source).

1. Define the goal.
2. Select the movement pattern.
3. Consider alignment and positioning options.
4. Focus on stabilization over movement.
5. Plan and control the tempo.
6. Integrate breathing control.
7. Perform a specific warm-up set for each exercise.

Body Weight Squat

This exercise is the first in a series of squat exercises. The squat exercise is a general movement pattern that transfers well to life demands and should help with the daily performance of getting up and down from chairs and picking up common objects such as boxes or bags. The variation presented here promotes more hip movement, less knee movement, and increased forward lean of the body to better target the glutes and to decrease knee stress. Other variations that emphasize more knee action can also be used if desired.

Target Muscles

Hip extensors (glutes, hamstrings, hip adductors), knee extensors (quadriceps), spinal extensors

Joint Motions

Hip extension, knee extension

Alignment and Positioning

1. Position the feet just outside shoulder width and angled out about 20 to 30 degrees, with the knees and hips slightly flexed.

2. Begin with the hands by the side, the shoulder blades pulled back, and the spine and head in good posture.

3. Exhale, activate the core, and contract the trunk, hip, and leg muscles to stabilize the starting position.

Motion and Stabilization

1. Slowly begin to inhale, push the hips back, and allow the knees to bend naturally and the trunk to lean forward.

2. Slowly raise the arms for counterbalance, and lower the body until the crest of the pelvis presses against the top of the thigh (or as far as possible) while maintaining proper posture and balance.

3. Hold, then slowly begin to exhale, activate the core, and press the body back up to the starting position while maintaining proper posture and pelvic positioning.

Balance Squat

This exercise is performed similarly to any squat exercise but has additional balance demands. The use of a balance device trains specific tilting-response reflexes that may be beneficial for certain goals. The long median plane fulcrum used in this demonstration tends to require increased hip adductor activity to correct for balance loss and stabilization. A frontal plane fulcrum, a round fulcrum, or other balance tools will provide different specific stability challenges for the ankles, hips, and trunk muscles. Remember to also include body-righting reflex training in any program targeting improved balance, and be sure to use the appropriate tools for the specific goals.

Target Muscles

Hip extensors (glutes, hamstrings, hip adductors), knee extensors (quadriceps), spinal extensors

Joint Motions

Hip extension, knee extension

Alignment and Positioning

1. Position the feet on the balance board just outside shoulder width and angled out about 20 to 30 degrees, with the knees and hips slightly flexed.

2. Begin with the hands by the side, the shoulder blades pulled back, and the spine and head in good posture.

3. Exhale, activate the core, and contract the trunk, hip, and leg muscles to stabilize the starting position.

Motion and Stabilization

1. Slowly begin to inhale, push the hips back, and allow the knees to bend naturally and the trunk to lean forward.

2. Slowly raise the arms for counterbalance, and lower the body until the crest of the pelvis presses against the top of the thigh (or as far as possible) while maintaining proper posture and balance.

3. Hold, then slowly begin to exhale, activate the core, and press the body back up to the starting position while maintaining proper posture and pelvic positioning.

Dumbbell Deadlift (Wide-Stance Squat)

This exercise is performed similarly to any squat movement, but a wider stance is used to allow the dumbbell and the arms to drop between the legs. This exercise targets the hip and knee extensors but also works posterior trunk muscles as stabilizers. It begins loading the squat in a manner very transferable to life demands. Most people must routinely perform this movement pattern in order to pick up a box, a container, or other miscellaneous objects. Heavy loads are difficult to perform with this exercise, because the dumbbell will tend to protract the scapula, which encourages flexion of the thoracic spine and reduces optimal posture.

Target Muscles

Hip extensors (glutes, hamstrings, hip adductors), knee extensors (quadriceps), spinal extensors

Joint Motions

Hip extension, knee extension

Dumbbell Deadlift (Wide-Stance Squat)

Alignment and Positioning

1. Position the feet well outside shoulder width and angled out about 30 to 45 degrees.

2. Squat and grasp the dumbbell with the arms straight and between the legs.

3. Begin in the squat position, with the hips and knees flexed and the trunk leaned forward in good posture. Draw a deep breath.

Motion and Stabilization

1. Slowly begin to exhale, activate the core, and press the body up by extending the hips and knees while pulling the shoulders back, keeping the dumbbell close to the legs.

2. Hold the top position, continue to exhale, further activate the core, and contract the trunk, hip, and leg muscles to stabilize.

3. Slowly begin to inhale, and squat back down, maintaining proper posture and pelvic positioning while lowering the dumbbell down (keeping it close to the legs) until back to the starting position.

Barbell Deadlift (Narrow-Stance Squat)

This exercise is similar to the traditional deadlift, except a modified starting position is used to reduce lumbar disc compression and lower back strain. All deadlifts are basically a squat movement challenging the hip and knee extensors and including high stabilization demands for the spinal extensors. The Barbell Deadlift utilizes a narrow stance as compared to the Dumbbell Deadlift and again places the load below the body's center of gravity. The deadlift transfers well to life's heavier lifting demands, but loads are limited by grip strength.

Target Muscles

Hip extensors (glutes, hamstrings, hip adductors), knee extensors (quadriceps), spinal extensors

Joint Motions

Hip extension, knee extension

Barbell Deadlift (Narrow-Stance Squat)

Alignment and Positioning

1. Set the barbell at the appropriate height to allow for the ability to maintain the natural lumbar curve and good posture.

2. Position the feet just inside shoulder width and pointed straight ahead. Grip the bar with a shoulder-width, alternate grip.

3. Begin in a squat position, with the hips and knees flexed and the trunk leaned forward in good posture. Draw a deep breath.

Motion and Stabilization

1. Slowly begin to exhale, activate the core, and press the body up by extending the hips and knees while pulling the shoulders back, keeping the bar close to the legs.

2. Hold the top position, continue to exhale, further activate the core, and contract the trunk, hip, and leg muscles to stabilize.

3. Slowly begin to inhale, and squat back down, maintaining proper posture and pelvic positioning while lowering the bar down (keeping it close to the legs) until back to the starting position.

Barbell Squat

This exercise maximally loads the squat movement and targets the hip and knee extensors. Bar placement on the upper back with the scapula retracted helps to stabilize the thoracic spine in an extended position, making posture easier to maintain under heavy loads and during long sets. In life, people may rarely place large loads on their backs to lift them, but all squats are considered general movement pattern training that transfers better to life demands than many other leg exercises. Individuals with neck, shoulder, and spinal stability concerns may need to consider other squat exercises.

Target Muscles

Hip extensors (glutes, hamstrings, hip adductors), knee extensors (quadriceps), spinal extensors

Joint Motions

Hip extension, knee extension

Alignment and Positioning

1. Place the barbell just above the scapula, with the hands placed comfortably on the bar and the elbows pointed down.

2. Position the feet just outside shoulder width and angled out about 20 to 30 degrees, with the knees and hips slightly flexed and the spine and head held in good posture.

3. Exhale, activate the core, and contract the trunk, hip, and leg muscles to stabilize the starting position.

Motion and Stabilization

1. Slowly begin to inhale, push the hips back, and allow the knees to bend naturally and the trunk to lean forward.

2. Lower the body until the crest of the pelvis presses against the top of the thigh (or as far as possible) while maintaining proper posture.

3. Hold, then slowly begin to exhale, activate the core, and press the body and barbell back up to the starting position while maintaining proper posture and pelvic positioning.

Machine Seated Leg Press

This exercise is good for targeting and strengthening the hip and knee extensors. Though not as transferable as a squat, leg pressing exercises may prove helpful for hypertrophy goals simply by adding more compound leg movement to a program. Small variations in feet positioning can be selected to better emphasize hip or knee extensor contribution. However, it is important to maintain the knee alignment and pelvic-spinal positioning described on page 93 to avoid additional risk of wear or injury to the knees or lower back area.

Target Muscles

Hip extensors (glutes, hamstrings, hip adductors), knee extensors (quadriceps)

Joint Motions

Hip extension, knee extension

Alignment and Positioning

1. Position the back pad and the feet in a manner that allows you to maintain an arch in the lower back and also prohibits the knees from passing too far over the toes.

2. For a wide stance, position the feet just outside shoulder width and angled out about 20 to 30 degrees. For a narrow stance, the feet should be at hip width and positioned straight.

3. Begin with a slight bend in the hips and knees, a natural arch in the lower back, and the core activated.

Motion and Stabilization

1. Slowly begin to inhale, and allow the legs and platform to lower until the thigh presses against the crest of the pelvis while maintaining the natural arch in the lower spine.

2. Hold, slowly begin to exhale, activate the core, and press the platform back to the starting position while maintaining the pelvic-spinal positioning described above.

3. Hold and stabilize the starting position; continue to maintain proper pelvic-spinal positioning and bend the knees slightly to avoid resting.

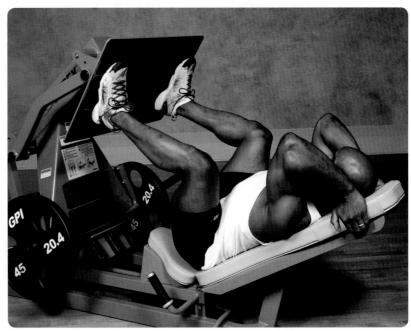

Body Weight Stationary Lunge

This exercise is good for beginning to strengthen the lunge movement. Lunges are similar to a single-leg squat, so they should be integrated into a program only after the squat has been mastered. This movement prepares the hip and leg muscles to stabilize and lift the body from an asymmetrical position. Such positions produce a torque on the pelvis, which brings additional hip, core, and trunk musculature into play to stabilize the body. The knee and MTP joints (joints of the toes) of the trail leg are also not in the best position to accept higher amounts of load, so positioning of the trunk, pelvis, and back leg is critical.

Target Muscles

Lead leg—hip extensors (glutes, hamstrings, hip adductors), knee extensors (quadriceps)

Joint Motions

Lead leg—hip extension, knee extension

Body Weight Stationary Lunge

Alignment and Positioning

1. Position the legs in a lunge position, with the lead leg far enough out to allow for the desired range of motion.

2. Straighten the back knee and lean forward so that the trunk is in line with the back leg while maintaining proper posture.

3. Begin with a slight bend in the lead hip and knee, a natural arch in the lower back, and the core activated.

Motion and Stabilization

1. Slowly begin to inhale, and allow the trunk to come forward and down until the crest of the pelvis presses against the top of the thigh (or as far as possible) while maintaining proper posture.

2. Be sure to keep the forward knee aligned straight with the toes, without letting it pass too far in front of the toes. Keep the trunk aligned with the back leg.

3. Hold, slowly begin to exhale, activate the core, and with the weight toward the heel, press the body back up to the starting position while maintaining good pelvic-spinal positioning.

Dumbbell Reverse Lunge

This exercise progresses the lunge from a stationary movement to a more dynamic movement. Since the lifter will be required to stabilize a single-leg position at certain points of the movement, this exercise will place a higher demand on the hip abductors as well as targeting the hip and knee extensors of the lead leg. Use of heavier dumbbells is difficult because they tend to protract the scapula and flex the thoracic spine, diminishing optimal posture. The use of a step (stair) is not necessary but can help to increase range of motion without having to step back as far.

Target Muscles

Lead leg—hip extensors (glutes, hamstrings, hip adductors), knee extensors (quadriceps), hip abductors

Joint Motions

Lead leg—hip extension, knee extension

Alignment and Positioning

1. Stand on a small step with most of your weight shifted to the lead leg, with the toe of the other leg just touching the step for balance.

2. Position the trunk in good posture, activate the core, and begin with the arms at the side.

3. Begin with a slight bend in the knee and hip of the lead leg, a natural arch in the lower back, and the core activated.

Motion and Stabilization

1. Begin to inhale, step back off the step, and lower the body so that the crest of the pelvis touches the top of the thigh of the lead leg, while keeping good posture.

2. Be sure to keep the forward knee aligned straight with the toes, without letting it pass too far in front of the toes. Keep the trunk aligned with the straight back leg.

3. Hold, slowly begin to exhale, activate the core, and with the weight toward the heel, press the body back up to the starting position while maintaining proper pelvic-spinal positioning.

Dumbbell Side Lunge

This exercise is simply a reverse lunge performed with a more lateral or diagonal movement. This increased lateral movement will demand more hip adductor recruitment to assist the hip and knee extensors of the lead leg. Use of heavier dumbbells tends to protract the scapula and flex the thoracic spine, diminishing optimal posture. The use of a step (stair) is not necessary but can help to increase range of motion without having to step as far back or out.

Target Muscles

Lead leg—hip extensors (glutes, hamstrings, hip adductors), knee extensors (quadriceps), hip abductors

Joint Motions

Lead leg—hip extension, knee extension

Alignment and Positioning

1. Stand on a small step with the lead foot and knee angled out about 20 to 30 degrees and the opposite foot just touching the step for balance.

2. Position the trunk in good posture, activate the core, and begin with the weighted arm slightly in front of the body.

3. Begin with a slight bend in the knee and hip of the lead leg, and with a natural arch in the lower back.

Motion and Stabilization

1. Begin to inhale, step off the step at a diagonal angle, and lower the body to a point where the crest of the pelvis presses against the top of the thigh of the lead leg, while maintaining good posture.

2. Be sure to keep the lead knee aligned straight with the toes, without letting it pass too far in front of the toes. Keep the trunk aligned with the straight back leg.

3. Hold, slowly begin to exhale, activate the core, and with the weight toward the heel, press the body back up to the starting position while maintaining proper posture.

Med Ball Traveling Lunge (Side Load)

This exercise further increases the balance and stability challenges because the movement is far more dynamic than a stationary or reverse lunge. The Med Ball is used for added resistance and may be more comfortable than using plates or dumbbells. The ball may be placed in front for a balanced anterior challenge, or to the side for an unbalanced lateral challenge. For heavier posterior loads, a barbell would probably work best. Choose the appropriate level and placement of loads to match your current abilities and specific goals. Typically, only light to moderate loads are needed for any traveling lunge because maximum strength development is not an appropriate goal for this exercise.

Target Muscles

Lead leg—hip extensors (glutes, hamstrings, hip adductors), knee extensors (quadriceps), hip abductors

Joint Motions

Lead leg—hip extension, knee extension

Med Ball Traveling Lunge (Side Load)

Alignment and Positioning

1. Stand with your weight on the lead leg and with the toes of the other leg just touching the ground for balance.

2. Position the ball on the shoulder, with the trunk in good posture. Activate the core and begin with a slight bend in the knee and hip of the lead leg.

Motion and Stabilization

1. Begin to inhale, lunge forward, and lean the trunk until the crest of the pelvis touches the top of the thigh of the lead leg (or as far as comfortable for the desired range of motion).

2. Be sure to keep the forward knee aligned straight with the toes, without letting it pass too far in front of the toes. Keep the trunk aligned with the straight back leg.

3. Hold, slowly begin to exhale, activate the core, and with the weight toward the heel, press the body forward and up to the starting position while maintaining proper posture. Repeat with the same leg or alternate if desired.

Barbell Hang Clean

This exercise is not designed for targeting muscles to achieve any aesthetic-based goal, but rather it is often selected for certain performance-based goals, such as improving plyometric actions of the hip and leg muscles and increasing combined lower body and trunk power. This movement requires a fast tempo or lifting speed and specific timing of various joint mechanics in order to obtain the desired benefits and reduce associated risks. Careful attention to technique and goal-to-risk assessment should be done before selecting this exercise or prescribing loads and volume.

Target Muscles

Ankle-knee-hip-trunk extensor chain, upper and mid trapezius, levator scapula

Joint Motions

Ankle extension, knee extension, hip extension, slight spinal extension, scapular elevation and retraction, shoulder abduction, shoulder external rotation

Barbell Hang Clean

Alignment and Positioning

1. Stand in good posture with the feet directly under the hips. Grasp the bar with an overhand grip, with the hands just outside shoulder-width apart.

2. Flex the hips and knees slightly to position the spine at an approximate 45-degree angle, with good posture and the bar close to the thighs. Draw a deep breath.

Motion and Stabilization

1. Quickly drop to a shallow squat, then immediately activate the core and quickly press off the ground with a jumping movement while pulling the shoulder blades and bar up.

2. Continue to extend the ankles, knees, and hips until the body is almost or just off the ground while continuing to pull the bar up to about chin level.

3. Quickly drop down under the bar while rotating the elbows and relaxing the wrists to catch the bar on the upper chest. Then front squat the weight to an upright position.

4. Quickly but cautiously flip the bar down to the starting position.

Dumbbell Snatch

This exercise is not designed for targeting muscles, but rather for targeting a movement to achieve specific performance-based goals. This exercise helps to improve plyometric actions of the hip and leg muscles and increases lower body and trunk extension power. This movement requires a fast tempo or lifting speed and specific timing of various joint mechanics in order to obtain the desired benefits and reduce associated risks. Careful attention to technique and goal-to-risk assessment should be done before selecting this exercise or prescribing loads and volume.

Target Muscles

Ankle-knee-hip-trunk extensor chain, shoulder flexors, scapular elevators, shoulder stabilizers

Joint Motions

Ankle extension, knee extension, hip extension, slight spinal extension, scapular elevation and retraction, shoulder flexion, shoulder external rotation

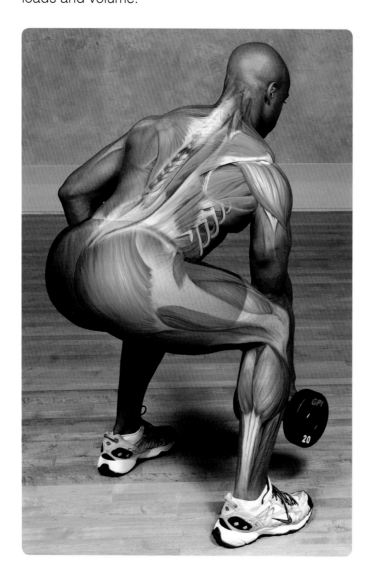

Alignment and Positioning

1. Place the feet just outside shoulder width, with the toes angled out about 10 to 20 degrees. Then squat and grasp the dumbbell between the legs.

2. Begin with the spine in good posture, a natural arch in the lower spine, and the knees aligned with the toes. Draw a deep breath.

Motion and Stabilization

1. Quickly squat slightly lower to prestretch the muscles, activate the core, and quickly press off the ground with a jumping movement while pulling the shoulder blades and dumbbell up and out.

2. Continue to extend the ankles, knees, and hips until the body is almost or just off the ground while continuing to pull the dumbbell out and up.

3. Allow the momentum of the dumbbell to carry it up and over the shoulder as you drop down slightly to position the body directly below it. Then squat the weight to an upright position.

4. Stabilize, then with two hands lower the dumbbell back to the floor. Then reposition and repeat.

Isolated Lower Body Exercises

In this chapter, several exercises that target and strengthen the pelvic, hip, and leg muscles of the lower body are presented. Integration of core and trunk muscle stabilization is an essential element of technique for many of these exercises. Exercise selections for the lower body can be classified in two general categories—compound exercises (such as squats, lunges, and presses) and isolated exercises for the ankles, knees, and hips. This chapter presents isolated leg movements that can also be classified as varied specific movement patterns. Lower body and pelvic structure and function, along with specific muscle physiology and biomechanical factors, were considered when developing the instructions for all elements of technique, such as alignment, positioning, motion, stabilization, and suggested breathing method.

These exercise selections vary in their difficulty of stabilization or movement demands in order to provide a well-balanced collection of movements to challenge individuals of all strength and fitness levels. Variations and modifications that will increase or decrease the level of challenge are also provided in the description section for many exercises. These additional suggestions combined with the information provided in the first three chapters should assist you in selecting the lower body exercises that best address your own performance and aesthetic goals. In addition to the abundant information on efficient exercise selection provided throughout this book, chapter 9 covers program design and will help you combine exercise selections into effective resistance training routines as well as assist you in designing long-term exercise programs. Remember to incorporate the elements of technique discussed in chapter 3 and summarized below. Consider them as steps or guidelines when selecting any of the exercises in this book (or from any other source).

1. Define the goal.
2. Select the movement pattern.
3. Consider alignment and positioning options.
4. Focus on stabilization over movement.
5. Plan and control the tempo.
6. Integrate breathing control.
7. Perform a specific warm-up set for each exercise.

Braced One-Leg Hip Flexion

This exercise targets strengthening of the hip flexor musculature, but it also challenges the core muscles and trunk flexors. The vertical positioning of the torso decreases core and trunk demand and thereby allows the lifter to better focus on the hip flexors. The straight-leg option increases the load and provides passive tension from the hamstrings and gastrocnemius that amplifies the challenge. This makes this exercise an active-stretching exercise for the hamstrings and calves as well as a strengthening exercise for the hip flexors. Double-leg, alternate-leg, and piston movements are variations that further increase the challenge, while bent-knee versions can be used to decrease the challenge.

Target Muscles

Hip flexors (psoas, iliacus, rectus femoris), core, spinal flexors

Joint Motions

Hip flexion

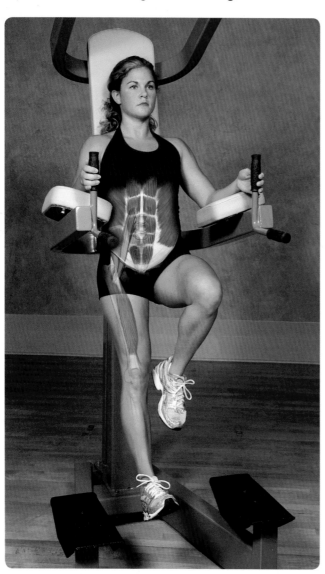

Alignment and Positioning

1. Brace the body on a hanging or Roman chair, with good posture, the elbows securely positioned under the shoulders, the scapula depressed, and the sacrum braced against the pad.

2. Begin with a full breath of air and with one leg positioned straight and just in front of the hips to create slight tension on the abdominal muscles. The other leg is bent so the thigh is about parallel to the ground.

Motion and Stabilization

1. Slowly begin to exhale, and activate the core muscles while raising the straight leg, keeping the knee locked and the ankle flexed back.

2. Continue to pull the leg up as high as possible. Then hold at the top position while maintaining proper posture and continuing to exhale and contract the core muscles and hip flexors.

3. Slowly begin to inhale, and lower the leg back down to the starting position while maintaining posture. Then repeat with the same leg or alternate with the other leg.

Swiss Ball Double-Leg Hip Flexion

This exercise targets strengthening the hip flexor musculature, and it also increases the challenge for the abdominal muscles and neck flexors. Using the Swiss ball places increased demand on the core and trunk muscles for balancing and stabilization. Single-leg and bent-knee versions are suggested before attempting the double-leg option. Increased loads can be implemented by simply adjusting the body farther out on the ball. Neck flexor strength is a prerequisite for this exercise, because the head cannot easily be rested at any time during the movement.

Target Muscles

Hip flexors (psoas, iliacus, rectus femoris), core, spinal flexors

Joint Motions

Hip flexion

Swiss Ball Double-Leg Hip Flexion

Alignment and Positioning

1. Lie supine on a Swiss ball, with good posture and the hands anchored on a stable object.

2. Begin with both legs up and straight, and with the ankles flexed.

3. Begin with the head and spine in good posture and the chin slightly tucked. Contract the core, abdominal, and hip flexor muscles.

Motion and Stabilization

1. Slowly begin to inhale, and lower the legs until the thighs are parallel with the body (or as low as possible) while maintaining posture and head position.

2. Hold at the bottom position, then slowly begin to exhale, activate the core, and pull the legs up to the starting position while maintaining head and spinal position.

3. Hold again at the top position, maintaining the straight leg and spinal positioning to actively stretch the hamstrings and calves while further contracting the core muscles. Then slowly inhale and repeat.

45-Degree Hip Extension

This exercise is designed to target the glutes and hamstring musculature and will also work the spinal erectors as stabilizers. Slight external rotation of the hips is presented on this exercise to further target the glutes but is not necessary or always advisable. Due to the knee being forced into a "locked position," people with knee concerns, larger people, or people with goals that require use of heavy additional loads may find that barbell and dumbbell hip extension exercises are better options.

Target Muscles

Hip extensors (glutes, hamstrings), spinal extensors, core

Joint Motions

Hip extension

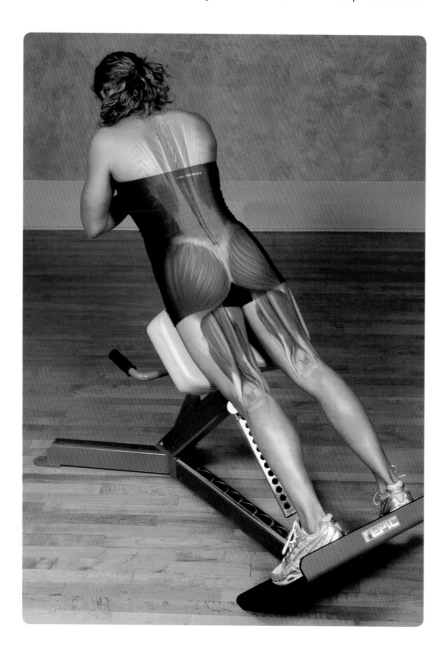

Alignment and Positioning

1. Position the brace so that the iliac spine of the pelvis will move freely over the pad. Then stand with the hips and feet straight and slightly externally rotated (about 30 degrees).

2. Retract the scapula and pull the arms slightly behind the torso, with the spine and head in good posture. (The arms may also be placed across the chest, behind the head, or overhead to further increase the load.)

3. Exhale, activate the core and abdominal muscles, and contract the glutes and hamstrings to stabilize the starting position.

Motion and Stabilization

1. Slowly begin to inhale, and lower the trunk as far as the hamstrings will allow while maintaining proper posture and head position.

2. Hold, slowly begin to exhale, activate the core, and pull the torso back up to the starting position by contracting the glutes and hamstrings. Continue to maintain head and spinal position.

3. Hold and stabilize this position, and finish exhaling while further contracting the core, glutes, and hamstrings.

Barbell Hip Extension

This exercise is designed to strengthen the glutes and hamstrings and will also train the spinal erectors as stabilizers. Using barbells, dumbbells, or other free weight loads in unsupported and standing positions allows the lifter to better load the exercise with less risk to the knees as compared to the 45-degree or other machine options. This lifting movement is also very transferable to life demands and can be considered a modified squat movement.

Target Muscles

Hip extensors (glutes, hamstrings), spinal extensors, core

Joint Motions

Hip extension

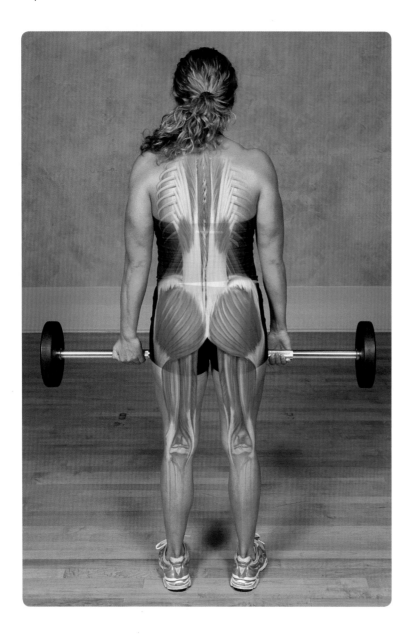

Alignment and Positioning

1. Position the feet straight ahead and directly under the hips, with the knees slightly bent.

2. Place the hands on the bar with an alternate grip, shoulder-width apart. Squat the bar up to the starting position, with the spine in good posture.

3. Begin from a standing position with the shoulders back and the spine and head in good posture. Exhale and activate the core to stabilize the starting position.

Motion and Stabilization

1. Slowly begin to inhale. Push the hips back and lower the trunk as low as the hamstrings will allow while maintaining proper posture and keeping the bar close to the body.

2. Hold at the bottom position. Then slowly begin to exhale, activate the core, and pull the torso back up to the starting position using the glutes and hamstrings while relaxing the arms and maintaining proper posture.

3. Hold and stabilize this position, and finish exhaling while further contracting the core, glutes, and hamstrings.

Dumbbell One-Leg Hip Extension

This exercise is designed not only to strengthen the glutes and hamstring musculature but also to train body-righting reflex actions and improve balance. Additional hip and ankle stabilizers of the stationary leg are also highly challenged with this exercise, along with the entire chain of spinal extensor muscles. This exercise is an advanced movement that targets the entire deep longitudinal subsystem. Individuals with limited hip mobility, tight hamstrings, ankle or spinal instability, or poor balance may initially need external assistance for this movement or may need to select another exercise altogether.

Target Muscles

Hip extensors (glutes, hamstrings), deep longitudinal subsystem (tibialis muscles, peroneus muscles, biceps femoris, sacrotuberal, ligament, spinal extensors), core

Joint Motions

Hip extension

Dumbbell One-Leg Hip Extension

Alignment and Positioning

1. Position the foot of the stationary leg straight ahead, and hold the other leg forward and up in a bent-knee position.

2. Hold the dumbbells relaxed at the side of the body. Balance and create good posture.

3. Begin with the shoulders back and the spine and head in good posture. Exhale and activate the core.

Motion and Stabilization

1. Slowly begin to inhale, and lower the leg down and back to straighten it while leaning the upper body over as far as the hamstrings will allow. Let the dumbbells lower, keeping them close to the body.

2. Continue to lean over and straighten the back leg while focusing on maintaining optimal posture and a level pelvic position.

3. Hold and balance. Then slowly begin to exhale, activate the core, and pull the leg and torso back up to the starting position using the glutes and hamstrings while maintaining proper posture.

Cable Hip Abduction

This exercise targets the gluteus medius and associated hip abductors. Hip abductors are important for pelvic stability, particularly when standing on one leg or for any walking, lunging, or running movements. Optimal gait performance and one-leg standing exercises rely on prior adequate hip abductor strength that may be best developed initially in an isolated manner, such as that presented with this exercise. Internal and external hip rotation may be added to better target specific regions of the hip abductors.

Target Muscles

Lateral subsystem (hip abductors—gluteus medius, gluteus minimus, tensor fascia latae; contralateral lateral trunk flexors—quadratus lumborum, internal obliques), core

Joint Motions

Hip abduction

Alignment and Positioning

1. Strap one cable to the outside ankle, and stand with the opposite foot straight ahead and the knee slightly bent.

2. Position the outside leg slightly across the body and in front of the stationary leg, and place the opposite hand lightly on the bar for balance assistance.

3. Begin with the shoulders back, the spine and head in good posture, and the pelvis level. Draw a deep breath.

Motion and Stabilization

1. Slowly begin to exhale, activate the core, and pull the leg across and out from the body while maintaining proper posture and pelvic position.

2. Hold this position and continue to contract the core, trunk, and hip abductors.

3. Slowly begin to inhale, and allow the leg to be pulled back to the starting position while maintaining proper posture and pelvic positioning.

Cable Hip Adduction

The hip adductors not only perform adduction but are also important synergists for hip extension and hip flexion. As such, these versatile muscles are also worked during any squatting or leg pressing movement as well as on certain hip flexion exercises. Therefore, the need for prior or additional isolated strengthening exercises for the hip adductors is not as great as for the hip abductors. However, this exercise may be valuable for specific rehabilitation or performance-related goals.

Target Muscles

Hip adductors (adductor magnus, adductor longus, adductor brevis, pectineus, gracilis), core, anterior oblique subsystem

Joint Motions

Hip adduction

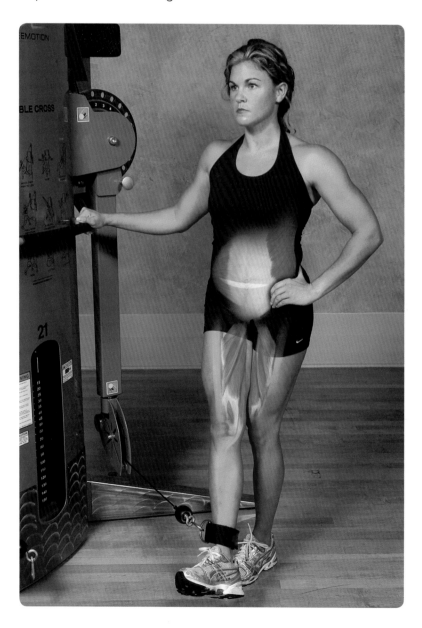

Alignment and Positioning

1. Strap one cable to the inside ankle, and stand with the opposite foot straight ahead, aligned directly under the hip, and with the knee slightly bent.

2. Begin with the movement leg about 45 degrees out from the body and the inside hand resting lightly on the bar for balance assistance.

3. Begin with the shoulders back, the spine and head in good posture, and the pelvis level. Draw a deep breath.

Motion and Stabilization

1. Slowly begin to exhale, activate the core, and pull the leg in and slightly across the body while maintaining proper posture and pelvic position.

2. Hold this position, and continue to exhale and to contract the core, trunk, and hip adductors.

3. Slowly begin to inhale, and allow the leg to be pulled back out to the starting position while maintaining proper posture and pelvic positioning.

Cable Quad Extension

This exercise loads the extension movement of the knee, targeting the quadriceps. However, the hip flexor of the movement leg, as well as the hip extensors and abductors of the stationary leg, will also be challenged as assistors and stabilizers. Core and trunk muscles will also be challenged to help stabilize the pelvis and spine. More or less stabilization from these muscles is required depending on the amount of arm use. An active stretch of the hamstrings and gas-trocnemius of the movement leg can also be accomplished with proper pelvic-spinal positioning and range of motion.

Target Muscles

Knee extensors (quadriceps), hip flexors, anterior oblique subsystem

Joint Motions

Hip flexion, knee extension

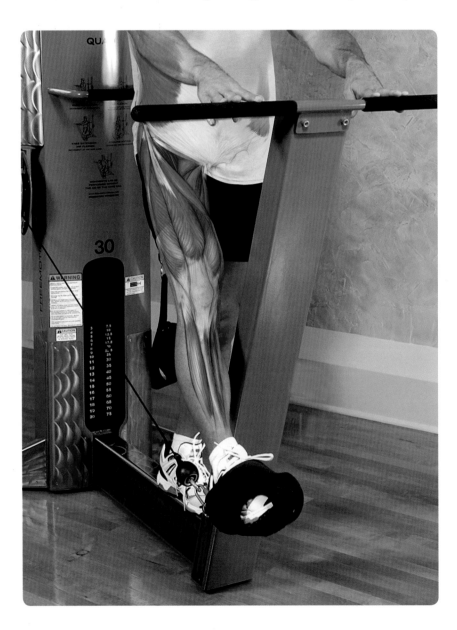

Alignment and Positioning

1. Stand with your weight on one leg and with the toe or ankle of the other leg in the strap, depending on the type of cable machine being used.

2. Begin with the movement leg slightly behind the stationary leg. Position the trunk in good posture.

3. Draw a deep breath, and begin with a slight bend in the hip and knee of the stationary leg.

Motion and Stabilization

1. Begin to exhale, activate the core, flex the hip to begin to pull the leg forward, and flex the ankle to pull the toes up.

2. Continue to pull the leg up, and begin extending the knee while maintaining posture and contracting the core and trunk muscles.

3. Hold, slowly begin to inhale, and allow the knee to bend and the leg to be pulled back to the starting position while maintaining posture.

Machine Quad Extension

This exercise isolates knee extension and directly loads the quadriceps muscles. This exercise may be used to accomplish hypertrophy goals, to prefatigue the quadriceps, to do rehabilitation work, or to simply add overall volume to a leg program. However, since the knee action is performed in a seated and completely externally stabilized position, the carryover strength and transference of this exercise are limited. Caution should be used when selecting the amount of resistance, because this machine places a direct shearing force across the knee proportional to the load.

Target Muscles

Knee extensors (quadriceps)

Joint Motions

Knee extension

Machine Quad Extension

Alignment and Positioning

1. Set the seat so that the knee joint is aligned with the axis and the pad is pressing against the shin.

2. Sit upright or lean against the back pad with good posture so that a full extension of the knee is not quite possible when maintaining the natural arch in the lower back. (Positioning is related to hamstring flexibility.)

3. Begin with the knee flexed no more than 90 degrees and aligned with the toes. Draw a deep breath.

Motion and Stabilization

1. Begin to exhale, activate the core, slightly flex the hips, and then begin to pull the lower legs up and the toes back.

2. Continue to pull the lower legs up and the toes back until the knees are almost locked (while maintaining good upper body posture), which should create a light stretch on the hamstrings.

3. Hold, then slowly inhale and allow the legs to be pulled down to the starting position while maintaining posture.

Cable Ham Flexion

This exercise loads hip extension along with knee flexion to better target the hamstrings and hip extensors of the movement leg. The hip flexors and hip abductors of the stationary leg are also challenged as stabilizers. Core and trunk muscles will also be challenged to help stabilize the pelvis and spine, with the amount depending on arm use and hand positioning. An active stretch of the hip flexor muscles of the movement leg can also be accomplished with proper hip positioning and technique.

Target Muscles

Knee flexors (hamstrings), hip extensors, posterior oblique subsystem

Joint Motions

Hip extension, knee flexion

Alignment and Positioning

1. Stand with your weight on one leg and with the foot or ankle of the other leg in the strap, depending on the machine being used.

2. Begin with the movement leg in front of the stationary leg. Position the trunk in good posture.

3. Draw a deep breath, and begin with a slight bend in the knee and hip of the stationary leg.

Motion and Stabilization

1. Begin to exhale, activate the core, begin to extend the hip by pulling the leg back, and stabilize the ankle.

2. Continue to pull the leg back and then flex the knee to about 90 degrees, causing a slight stretch on the hip flexors, while maintaining good posture and further activating the core.

3. Hold, then slowly inhale and allow the leg to be pulled back to the starting position while maintaining posture.

Machine Ham Flexion

This exercise isolates knee flexion and directly targets the hamstring muscles. This exercise may be helpful for achieving hypertrophy goals, working on isolated strengthening of the hamstrings, or simply adding overall volume to a leg program. Knee extension is a resisted movement in squats, presses, and lunges, so a certain amount of isolated knee flexion may be needed to help balance overall strength of the knees. However, isolated joint movements performed in externally stabilized environments have little transference to life uses. Caution should be used when selecting the amount of resistance and prescribing the volume for these types of exercises.

Target Muscles

Knee flexors (hamstrings)

Joint Motions

Knee flexion

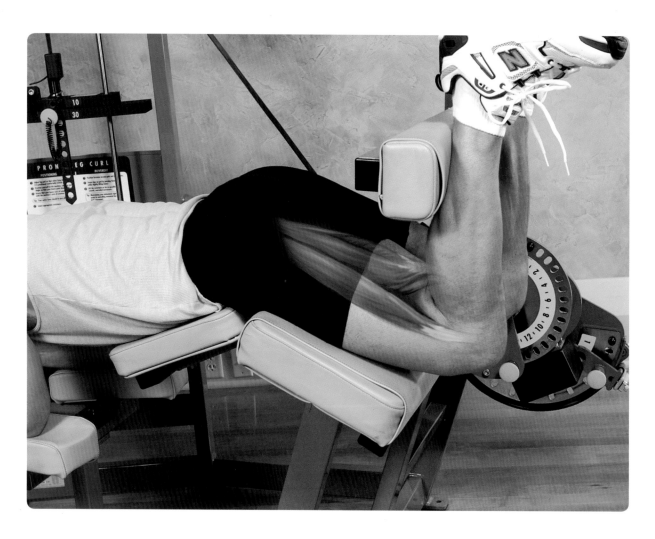

Alignment and Positioning

1. Lie prone on a bench so that the knee joint is aligned with the axis and the pad is positioned below the gastrocnemius and above the Achilles tendon.

2. Position the trunk and neck in proper posture, with the head off the pad looking straight down and with the chin tucked.

3. Begin with the knees slightly bent, the pelvis pressed against the pad, and the feet straight and stabilized. Draw a deep breath.

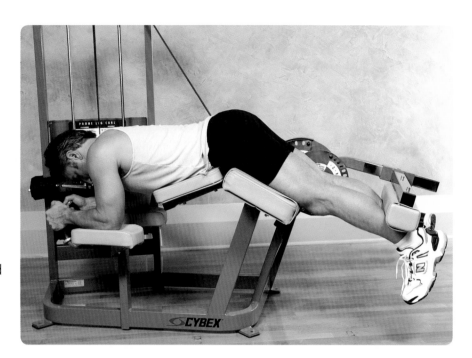

Motion and Stabilization

1. Begin to exhale, activate the core, press the pelvis tight into the pad (slightly raising the knees off the pad), and begin to pull the lower legs up.

2. Continue to slightly lift the knees, and pull the lower legs up so that the knee is flexed about 90 degrees while maintaining posture and further contracting the core and trunk muscles.

3. Hold, then slowly inhale and allow the legs to be pulled down to the starting position while maintaining pelvic-spinal positioning.

Dumbbell One-Leg Calf Extension

This exercise is an often overlooked option for training the ankle extensors and is more transferable to life demands than machine calf extension movements. The amount of balance challenge can be moderated by using a hand to assist. Options for strengthening ankle eversion or inversion are also available with this exercise through voluntary ankle control that is not possible when using most machines.

Target Muscles

Ankle extensors (triceps surae)

Joint Motions

Ankle extension (plantar flexion)

Dumbbell One-Leg Calf Extension

Alignment and Positioning

1. Stand in good posture with the ball of one foot securely positioned on a step, with the toes and entire leg pointed straight ahead. The other leg should be slightly bent.

2. Hold a dumbbell in the opposite or same-side arm depending on the degree of balance challenge desired. Place the opposite hand lightly on a wall or stable object for slight balance assistance.

3. Begin with a slight bend in the knee, the ankle flexed, and the heel just below the ball of the foot. Then inhale.

Motion and Stabilization

1. Begin to exhale, activate the core, and extend the ankle to lift the body up, keeping the ankle from rolling out and the weight over the ball of the foot.

2. Extend the ankle as far as possible, keeping it stable and lifting the body while maintaining good posture and further contracting the core and trunk muscles.

3. Hold, then slowly inhale and allow the body to lower down to the starting position while maintaining proper posture and ankle positioning.

Machine Calf Extension

This exercise can be used to isolate ankle extension and better load the calves. This exercise may be helpful for achieving hypertrophy goals, working on specific ankle strengthening, or if using this particular machine, concurrently strengthening ankle inversion or eversion along with ankle extension. Though beneficial for certain aesthetic- or performance-based goals, isolated machine training exercises may not transfer much to meeting the demands placed on the ankle during life situations or during higher speed dynamic movements. This exercise can also be done with one leg at a time for isolateral strengthening of the ankles.

Target Muscles

Ankle extensors (triceps surae)

Joint Motions

Ankle extension (plantar flexion)

Machine Calf Extension

Alignment and Positioning

1. Sit with the balls of the feet securely positioned on the foot pedals, with the toes and legs aligned straight.

2. Pull the shoulders back, position the spine in good posture, and draw a deep breath.

3. Begin with a slight bend in the knees, and flex the ankles so that the heels are slightly in front of the balls of the feet.

Motion and Stabilization

1. Begin to exhale, activate the core, and extend the ankles to press the foot pedals out while maintaining pelvic-spinal positioning.

2. Press the pedals out as far as possible while keeping the ankles from rolling in or out. Keep the pressure through the balls of the feet, and further contract the core and trunk muscles.

3. Hold, then slowly inhale and allow the ankles to flex and the pedals to return to the starting position while maintaining good posture.

Machine Bent-Leg Calf Extension

This exercise targets strengthening of the ankle extensors, with emphasis placed primarily on the soleus. Because the gastrocnemius muscles are two-joint muscles, when bending the knee they are preshortened and become active insufficient, leaving the soleus to carry most of the load. With any calf exercise, you should avoid having the weight force the ankles to flex more than they could actively flex on their own power. This exercise may be helpful for achieving certain aesthetic-based or performance-based goals, but it will transfer little to the life demands regularly placed on the ankles.

Target Muscles

Ankle extensors (triceps surae)

Joint Motions

Ankle extension (plantar flexion)

Machine Bent-Leg Calf Extension

Alignment and Positioning

1. Sit with the balls of the feet securely positioned on the step, with the toes and legs aligned straight ahead.

2. Place the knees under the pads, pull the shoulders back, and position the spine in good posture.

3. Begin with the heels slightly below the balls of the feet. Draw a deep breath.

Motion and Stabilization

1. Begin to exhale, activate the core, and extend the ankles to lift the knees and the weight.

2. Press up as far as possible, keeping the ankles from rolling out and keeping the weight over the balls of the feet. Continue to contract the core and trunk muscles.

3. Hold, then slowly inhale and allow the legs to lower down to the starting position while maintaining proper posture and ankle positioning.

Machine Tib Flexion

This exercise isolates strengthening of the ankle flexors, emphasizing the tibialis anterior. Strengthening exercises are often performed for the ankle extensors in training programs, but these important flexors of the ankle are often overlooked. Maintaining a relative strength balance around any joint is a key for optimal performance of the joint and for decreasing the risk of potential injury. This exercise may also serve as an active-stretching exercise of the gastrocnemius and Achilles tendon when done properly and with a full concentric range of motion.

Target Muscles

Ankle flexors (tibialis anterior), flexor digitorums, flexor hallucis

Joint Motions

Ankle flexion (dorsiflexion)

Alignment and Positioning

1. Stand with the foot placed securely under the pad, with the ankle aligned with the axis of the machine.

2. Straighten and lock the knee of the working leg, and position the foot parallel to the ground.

3. Stand in good posture while balancing on one leg. Draw a deep breath.

Motion and Stabilization

1. Begin to exhale, activate the core, and flex the ankle to pull the foot up and back.

2. Flex the ankle as far as possible while keeping the toes relaxed and the knee locked. Further contract the core and trunk muscles.

3. Hold, then slowly inhale and allow the foot to lower down to the starting position while maintaining proper posture and ankle positioning.

Upper Body Pushing Exercises

In this chapter, several exercises are presented that target and strengthen the scapular, shoulder, elbow, and wrist muscles that are responsible for providing pushing forces. Integration of core and trunk muscle stabilization is an essential element of technique for many of these exercises. Pushing exercises are classified as general movement patterns, but some specific movement patterns that are used for isolating the triceps (which assist in pushing movements) are also included in this chapter. Upper body structure and function, along with specific muscle physiology and all biomechanical factors, were considered when developing the instructions for all elements of technique, such as alignment, positioning, motion, stabilization, and suggested breathing method.

These exercise selections vary in their difficulty of stabilization or movement demands in order to provide a well-balanced collection of movements to challenge individuals of all strength and fitness levels. Variations and modifications that will increase or decrease the level of challenge are also provided in the description section for many exercises. These additional suggestions combined with the information provided in the first three chapters should assist you in selecting the upper body exercises that best address your own performance and aesthetic goals. In addition to the abundant information on efficient exercise selection provided throughout this book, chapter 9 covers program design and will help you combine exercise selections into effective resistance training routines as well as assist you in designing long-term exercise programs. Remember to incorporate the elements of technique discussed in chapter 3 and summarized below. Consider them as steps or guidelines when selecting any of the exercises in this book (or from any other source).

1. Define the goal.
2. Select the movement pattern.
3. Consider alignment and positioning options.
4. Focus on stabilization over movement.
5. Plan and control the tempo.
6. Integrate breathing control.
7. Perform a specific warm-up set for each exercise.

Dumbbell and Bench Chest Press

This exercise is a horizontal plane press that targets the chest and anterior shoulder muscles. Dumbbells provide for more freedom of movement, require more demand from scapular and shoulder stabilizers, and reduce some of the additional shearing and compressive forces associated with barbell and machine presses. Dumbbells also allow more user options for accomplishing different goals, such as unilateral movements, alternate movements, piston movements, or using different loads in each hand. This exercise is presented with a retracted scapular positioning to decrease stress on the shoulder joint, because natural scapular movement and rhythm are not possible while on a bench.

Target Muscles

Sternal pectoralis major, clavicular pectoralis major, anterior deltoid, triceps

Joint Motions

Shoulder horizontal flexion, elbow extension

Dumbbell and Bench Chest Press

Alignment and Positioning

1. Lie supine on a bench, with good posture, a natural arch in the lower spine, and the feet braced firmly on the floor or on a step.

2. Retract the shoulder blades slightly together, and position the dumbbells horizontal to the body and aligned over the shoulders.

3. Begin with the elbows pointed outward, the wrists straight, and the core and trunk muscles contracted.

Motion and Stabilization

1. Begin to inhale. Slowly lower the arms and allow the hands to separate, keeping them just inside the elbows, while maintaining pelvic-spinal positioning.

2. Continue to lower the arms until the upper arm is about parallel with the floor, with the hands slightly inside the elbows.

3. Hold, slowly exhale, activate the core, and press the arms and dumbbells back to the starting position while maintaining proper posture and scapular positioning.

Barbell and Bench Chest Press

This exercise targets the chest, shoulder, and triceps muscles. Pressing with a barbell forces a closed-chain action of the arms that may enable the lifter to move heavier loads than with dumbbells but also inherently adds shearing and compressive forces that can stress and increase wear on the shoulder joints. These forces are further increased when using improper hand positioning, increased range of motion, faster tempos, and heavier loads. Technique, goal determination, and risk-to-benefit assessment should be carefully considered when selecting loads and prescribing volume for this exercise.

Target Muscles

Sternal pectoralis major, clavicular pectoralis major, anterior deltoid, triceps

Joint Motions

Shoulder horizontal flexion, elbow extension

Barbell and Bench Chest Press

Alignment and Positioning

1. Lie supine on a bench, with good posture and with the feet braced firmly on the floor or on a step.

2. Retract the shoulder blades slightly together, and place the hands on the bar at a width that will create a 90-degree angle at the elbow when the upper arm is parallel to the floor.

3. Begin with the bar over the chest, the elbows pointed out, the wrists straight, and the core and trunk muscles contracted.

Motion and Stabilization

1. Begin to inhale. Slowly lower the arms and the bar while keeping the elbows under the bar and maintaining pelvic-spinal positioning.

2. Continue to lower the bar down until the upper arm is about parallel with the floor, with the hands just inside the elbows.

3. Hold, slowly begin to exhale, activate the core, and press the arms and the barbell back to the starting position while maintaining proper posture and scapular positioning.

Dumbbell and Swiss Ball One-Arm Incline Chest Press

This exercise targets the upper chest and anterior shoulder muscles. By working on a less stable surface and unequally loading the body, it places an additional demand on the core, trunk rotators, and associated hip muscles to maintain proper posture against the applied rotational force. Exercises done on the ball also require more neck flexor strength because the head will be unsupported throughout the exercise. This exercise can be done at different body and shoulder angles for more or less chest emphasis. It can also be performed with two arms, alternate movements, piston movements, or with different weight in each hand for varied training effects.

Target Muscles

Sternal pectoralis major, clavicular pectoralis major, anterior deltoid, triceps

Joint Motions

Shoulder horizontal to frontal plane flexion, elbow extension

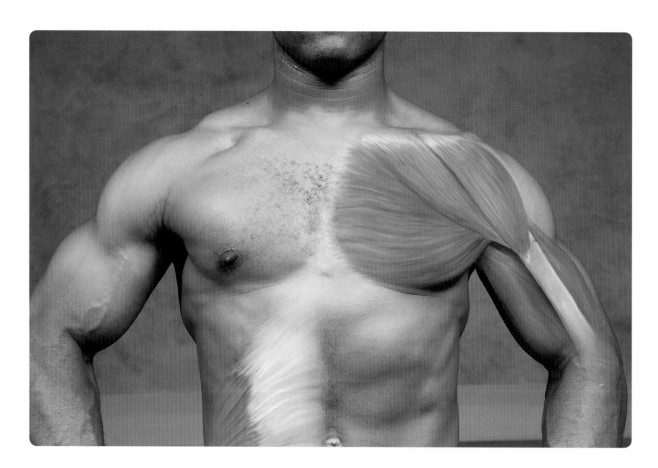

Dumbbell and Swiss Ball One-Arm Incline Chest Press

Alignment and Positioning

1. Position the body at a 45-degree angle on a Swiss ball, with good posture and with the feet braced firmly on the floor or on a step.

2. Pull the shoulders slightly together, and position the dumbbell horizontal to the body and aligned straight over the shoulder.

3. Begin with the elbow pointed out, the wrist straight, and the core and trunk muscles contracted.

Motion and Stabilization

1. Begin to inhale, and lower the arm while keeping the hand slightly inside the elbow and avoiding any rotation of the trunk.

2. Continue to lower the arm until the upper arm is about parallel with the floor, with the hand slightly inside the elbow. Maintain good posture.

3. Hold, slowly exhale, activate the core, and press the arm and dumbbell back to the starting position while maintaining proper posture.

Cable One-Arm Decline Chest Press

This exercise targets the lower chest and anterior shoulder muscles. Pressing with one arm while in the lunge position also targets the same-side obliques, associated core and abdominal muscles, and the contralateral hip adductors and flexors, which can collectively be considered the anterior oblique subsystem (AOS). This exercise may not be a high contributor for achieving certain aesthetic goals, such as chest hypertrophy, but it is valuable for addressing performance-related goals such as improved pelvic-spinal stabilization or preparation for powerful rotational movements. This should be a prerequisite for the Cable Trunk Rotation With Press exercise presented in chapter 4.

Target Muscles

Sternal pectoralis major, clavicular pectoralis major, anterior deltoid, triceps, anterior oblique subsystem

Joint Motions

Shoulder horizontal flexion, elbow extension

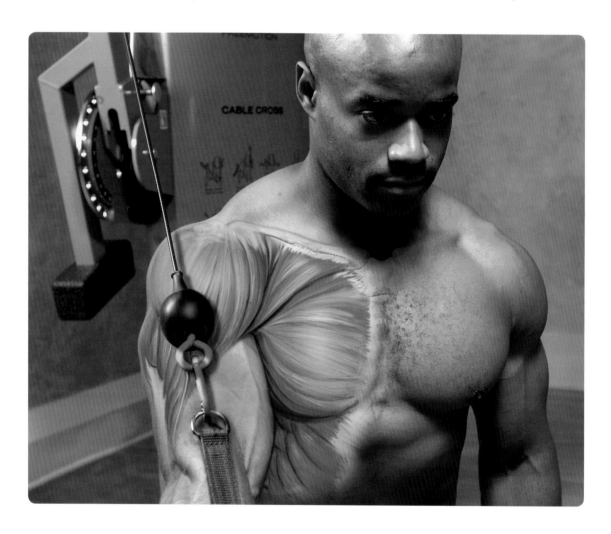

Cable One-Arm Decline Chest Press

Alignment and Positioning

1. Stand in a lunge position, with the feet about shoulder-width apart and the trunk leaned forward in good posture.

2. Position the cable handle down, perpendicular to the body, and aligned straight with the shoulder and pulley.

3. Begin with the elbow straight and pointed out, the wrist straight, and the core and trunk muscles contracted.

Motion and Stabilization

1. Begin to inhale, and slowly allow the arm to be pulled out and up while keeping the hand slightly inside the elbow and avoiding any movement of the trunk.

2. Continue to have the arm pulled back until the elbow is about even with the shoulder, with the hand slightly inside the elbow.

3. Hold, slowly exhale, activate the core, and press the arm back down and in to the starting position while maintaining proper posture.

Squat Rack Push-Up

This exercise also targets the chest, shoulder, and triceps muscles. Performing push-ups forces the same closed-chain action that occurs with a barbell press and can be stressful to the shoulder joints; this can be compounded with certain hand positioning and alignment options. The push-up position also places a load on the abdominal and hip flexors for stabilization requirements. Challenge can be decreased or increased by raising or lowering the angle of the body before beginning. Performing a push-up with one foot off the ground increases balance challenge and increases the load on the hip flexor of the stationary leg.

Target Muscles

Sternal pectoralis major; clavicular pectoralis major; anterior deltoid; triceps; core, trunk, and hip flexors

Joint Motions

Shoulder horizontal flexion, elbow extension

Alignment and Positioning

1. Position the bar at the desired height for the appropriate resistance. Place the hands at a width that will form a 90-degree angle at the elbow when the upper arm is parallel to the floor.

2. Align the body at a perpendicular angle to the arms, with the balls of the feet firmly pressed against the floor.

3. Begin with good posture, the elbows pointed out, the wrists straight, and the core and trunk muscles contracted.

Motion and Stabilization

1. Begin to inhale, and allow the body to lower while keeping the elbows pointed out and the spine and pelvis stabilized.

2. Continue to lower the body down until an approximate 90-degree angle is formed at the elbow.

3. Hold, slowly exhale, activate the core, and press the body back up to the starting position while maintaining proper posture.

Dumbbell Median Plane Shoulder Press

This exercise targets the anterior deltoids but also works some upper chest muscles and the triceps. The median plane is the most common plane a person moves in throughout the day. However, pushing exercises in the median plane are often neglected in resistance training programs. This exercise can be performed at a variety of body angles depending on the lifter's active range of motion abilities. This exercise is presented with a stabilized scapular position because natural scapular movement and rhythm are not possible when braced against a bench.

The exercise can also be performed with a single arm, alternate movements, piston movements, and offset loads for varied training effects.

Target Muscles

Anterior deltoids, clavicular pectoralis major, triceps

Joint Motions

Shoulder median flexion, elbow extension

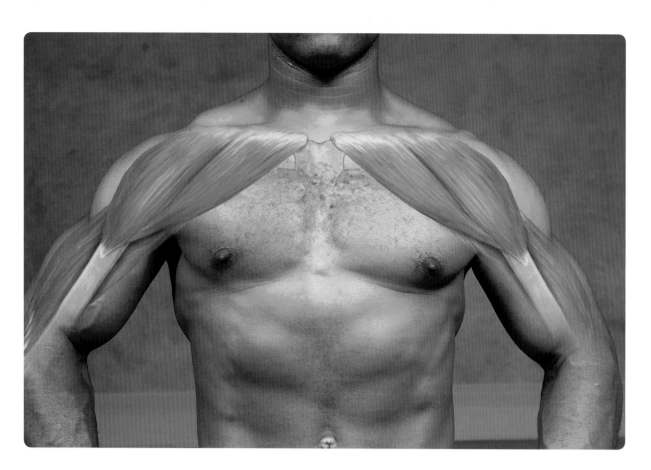

Dumbbell Median Plane Shoulder Press

Alignment and Positioning

1. Position the body with good posture on a bench at a 30- to 80-degree angle depending on shoulder mobility and desired goals.

2. Begin with the dumbbells parallel to the body and just over the elbows, which are also aligned parallel to the body.

3. Slightly retract and depress the shoulder blades, lift the chest, and create a natural arch in the lower back. Draw a deep breath.

Motion and Stabilization

1. Begin to exhale, activate the core, and slowly press the arms up, keeping the dumbbells and the elbows aligned parallel with the body.

2. Continue to press the arms up until directly over the shoulders while maintaining pelvic-spinal and scapular positioning.

3. Hold, then slowly begin to inhale, and lower the arms back to the starting position while maintaining proper posture.

Dumbbell Frontal Plane Shoulder Press

This exercise targets the anterior shoulder, the triceps, and, to a lesser extent, the upper chest. However, frontal plane pressing requires specific scapular-thoracic and scapular-humeral rhythm that subsequently integrates serratus anterior, levator scapula, and trapezius muscles as well. The trunk is not braced against a bench for this exercise in order to allow for proper scapular motion. Therefore it requires increased core, trunk, and hip musculature to meet balance and stabilization demands. This exercise can be performed with alternate movements, piston movements, offset loads, or with one arm for varied goals.

Target Muscles

Anterior deltoids, clavicular pectoralis major, triceps, trapezius, other scapular upward rotators

Joint Motions

Shoulder frontal flexion, elbow extension

Dumbbell Frontal Plane Shoulder Press

Alignment and Positioning

1. Sit in good posture with the hips and knees flexed about 90 degrees and a natural arch in the lower back.

2. Bring the arms up and out to the side of the body, with the upper arms about parallel to the floor, the elbows flexed about 90 degrees, and with the dumbbells level and just inside the elbows.

3. Slightly lift the chest, stabilize posture, and inhale.

Motion and Stabilization

1. Begin to exhale, activate the core, and slowly press the arms up, keeping the dumbbells and the elbows aligned with the body.

2. Continue to press the arms up and over until directly over the shoulders. Attempt to elevate the shoulder blades as they rotate upward while maintaining pelvic-spinal positioning.

3. Hold, then slowly begin to inhale, and lower the arms back to the starting position while maintaining proper posture.

Dumbbell One-Arm and One-Leg Frontal Plane Shoulder Press

This exercise targets the anterior shoulder, the triceps, and, to a lesser extent, the upper chest. However, frontal plane pressing requires specific scapular-thoracic and scapular-humeral rhythm that subsequently integrates trapezius and other scapular muscles as well. The single-leg positioning demands high levels of involvement for the core, trunk, and hip muscles to stabilize the body, particularly those muscles that make up the lateral subsystem (LS). This exercise can also be performed using the opposite arm, both arms, offset loads, or alternate and piston movements for varied training effects.

Target Muscles

Anterior deltoids, clavicular pectoralis major, triceps, trapezius, other scapular upward rotators, lateral subsystem (hip abductors, contralateral trunk lateral flexors)

Joint Motions

Shoulder frontal flexion, elbow extension

Dumbbell One-Arm and One-Leg Frontal Plane Shoulder Press

Alignment and Positioning

1. Stand on one leg, with the other foot off the ground. Position the pelvis level and the trunk in good posture.

2. Bring the arm up and out to the side of the body, with the upper arm about parallel to the floor, the elbow flexed about 90 degrees, and the dumbbell level and just inside the elbow.

3. Slightly lift the chest, stabilize posture, and inhale.

Motion and Stabilization

1. Begin to exhale, activate the core, and slowly press the arm up, keeping the dumbbell and the elbow aligned with the body.

2. Continue to press the arm up and over until directly over the shoulder. Attempt to elevate the shoulder blade as it rotates upward while maintaining pelvic-spinal positioning.

3. Hold, then slowly begin to inhale, and lower the arm back to the starting position while maintaining proper posture.

Cable One-Arm 90-Degree Triceps Extension

This exercise targets the triceps muscle group. The flexed shoulder position helps to emphasize the long head of the triceps, and the neutral elbow positioning will target wrist adductors. Performing this exercise in a standing, unbraced position also places a stabilization demand on the core, trunk, and hip muscles. Although isolated elbow extension is most often associated with aesthetic goals, the specific shoulder, elbow, and wrist positioning and the trunk stabilization challenges may help to concurrently progress certain performance goals as well. Two-arm, alternate, and piston movements may be possible options if using certain brands of pulley and cable machines with dual handles.

Target Muscles

Triceps, wrist adductors, shoulder and scapular stabilizers

Joint Motions

Elbow extension

Cable One-Arm 90-Degree Triceps Extension

Alignment and Positioning

1. Hold the handle of the upper cable lengthwise in the hand, and step out into a lunge position.

2. Lean the trunk over to approximately a 45-degree angle, and position the elbow and shoulder at about 90-degree angles, with the lower arm and hand in a neutral position.

3. Begin with the entire spine and neck in good posture. Draw a deep breath.

Motion and Stabilization

1. Begin to exhale, activate the core, and contract the triceps to begin extending the elbow.

2. Continue to fully extend the elbow, keeping the shoulder, scapula, and wrist stabilized and keeping the elbow pointed to the floor.

3. Hold, then slowly inhale and allow the lower arm to be pulled back to the starting position, keeping the shoulder, scapula, and wrist stabilized and the trunk in good posture.

Cable Zero-Degree Triceps Extension

This exercise emphasizes the lateral head of the triceps by using a shoulder position that preshortens the long head of the triceps, making it somewhat active insufficient toward the end of the range of motion. This exercise is often selected primarily for aesthetic-based goals. However, it does require a significant level of stabilization to maintain the recommended scapular depression, scapular retraction, and spinal positioning that will improve postural ability as well as develop the triceps. Note that a curved bar can be used to position the lower arms in a semineutral position that makes it easier to stabilize proper shoulder positioning, which assists with posture and decreases elbow stress.

Target Muscles

Triceps, shoulder and scapular stabilizers

Joint Motions

Elbow extension

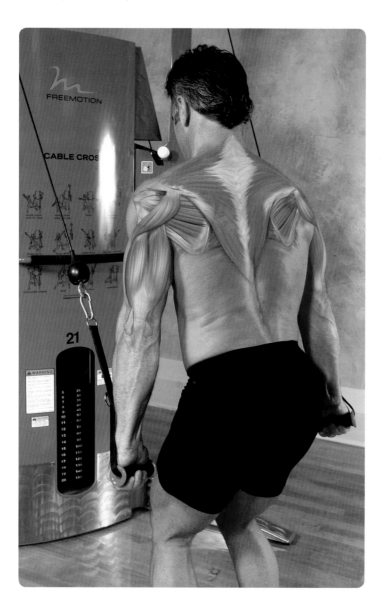

Cable Zero-Degree Triceps Extension

Alignment and Positioning

1. Face the cable column, and grasp the handles with the hands about shoulder-width apart and in a semi-neutral position.

2. Lean the trunk forward in good posture, flexing at the hips as needed to be aligned parallel with the cable.

3. Pull the elbows to the side so they are parallel to the body, pointed down, and flexed about 120 degrees. Stabilize the shoulders and inhale.

Motion and Stabilization

1. Begin to exhale, activate the core, and contract the triceps to begin extending the elbows.

2. Continue to fully extend the elbows, keeping the shoulders, scapula, and wrists stabilized and keeping the elbows pointed back.

3. Hold, then slowly inhale and allow the lower arms to be pulled back to the starting position, keeping the shoulders, scapula, and wrists stabilized and the trunk in good posture.

Upper Body Pulling Exercises

In this chapter, several exercises are presented that target and strengthen the scapular, shoulder, elbow, and wrist muscles that are involved in providing pulling forces. Integration of core and trunk muscle stabilization is an essential element of technique for many of these exercises. Pulling exercises are classified as general movement patterns, but some specific movement patterns that are used for isolating various pulling muscles to accomplish a variety of possible training goals are also included in this chapter. Upper body structure and function, along with specific muscle physiology and all biomechanical factors, were considered when developing the instructions for all elements of technique, such as alignment, positioning, motion, stabilization, and suggested breathing method.

These exercise selections vary in their difficulty of stabilization or movement demands in order to provide a well-balanced collection of movements to challenge individuals of all strength and fitness levels. Variations and modifications that increase or decrease the level of challenge are also provided in the description section for many exercises. These additional suggestions combined with the information provided in the first three chapters should assist you in selecting the upper body exercises that best address your own performance and aesthetic goals. In addition to the abundant information on efficient exercise selection provided throughout this book, chapter 9 covers program design and will help you combine all exercise selections into effective resistance training routines as well as assist you in designing long-term exercise programs. Remember to incorporate the elements of technique discussed in chapter 3 and summarized below. Consider them as steps or guidelines when selecting any of the exercises in this book (or from any other source).

1. Define the goal.
2. Select the movement pattern.
3. Consider alignment and positioning options.
4. Focus on stabilization over movement.
5. Plan and control the tempo.
6. Integrate breathing control.
7. Perform a specific warm-up set for each exercise.

Cable Seated Low Lat Row

This exercise targets the lats and scapular retractors, and it works the rear deltoids and biceps as well. In addition, the direct pull of the resistance against the trunk challenges the spinal erectors and associated posterior trunk and core muscles. Rowing exercises are pulling movements that can be performed at different angles in the median plane. They provide maximal shortening of the lats and train the spinal and scapular muscles necessary for optimal posture. Therefore, rowing exercises are good selections for both aesthetic- and performance-based goals. Proper posture is imperative for this exercise to prevent excessive stress on the lumbar spinal structures.

Target Muscles

Latissimus dorsi, posterior deltoids, scapular retractors, spinal extensors

Joint Motions

Scapular retraction, shoulder median extension, elbow flexion

Alignment and Positioning

1. Grab the handles or a bar using a neutral grip with the hands parallel to the body.

2. Sit with the legs about shoulder-width apart and the knees bent as needed to allow for a natural arch in the lower back.

3. Begin with the arms straight, the scapula neutral to slightly protracted, and the spine in good posture. Then inhale.

Motion and Stabilization

1. Begin to exhale, activate the core, and start to pull the shoulder blades together while pulling the arms down and back.

2. Continue to retract the scapula, and pull the arms back until the elbows are aligned with the shoulders (or as far as possible) while maintaining proper posture.

3. Hold, slowly inhale, and allow the arms and scapula to be pulled back to the starting position while maintaining proper posture.

Dumbbell Lat Row

This exercise targets the lats and scapular retractors, and it works the rear deltoids and biceps as well. In addition, the vertical pull of the resistance against the trunk places a high stabilization demand on the spinal and hip extensors. This and similar free weight exercises require a high level of hamstring flexibility in order to position the trunk in opposition to gravity and maintain a natural lumbar curvature. Using cable-pulley systems for standing rowing movements may be a better option if hip mobility and spinal sta-bility are not yet adequate. One-arm braced or unbraced positions and alternate or piston movements are optional variations.

Target Muscles

Latissimus dorsi, posterior deltoids, scapular retractors, spinal extensors, hip extensors

Joint Motions

Scapular retraction, shoulder median extension, elbow flexion

Dumbbell Lat Row

Alignment and Positioning

1. Hold the dumbbells with a neutral grip, and stand with the legs set just inside shoulder width.

2. Flex the hips, slightly bend the knees, and lean the upper body over until the trunk is close to parallel with the floor while maintaining good posture and a natural arch in the lower spine.

3. Begin with the dumbbells parallel to the body, the hands slightly in front of the shoulders, and the spine in good posture. Draw a deep breath.

Motion and Stabilization

1. Begin to exhale, activate the core, and start to pull the shoulder blades together while pulling the arms back and up.

2. Continue to retract the scapula and maintain posture. Pull the arms up and back, keeping the dumbbells outside the thighs, until the upper arms are about parallel to the body and the hands are under the navel.

3. Hold, slowly inhale, and allow the arms and scapula to be pulled back to the starting position while maintaining proper posture.

Cable One-Arm Low Lat Row

This exercise targets the lats, scapular retractors, rear deltoids, and biceps. Pulling with one arm while in the lunge position also places a rotational force across the pelvis and spine that will require the glutes of the lead leg and other associated hip and trunk musculature of the posterior oblique subsystem (POS) for stabilization. This exercise is valuable for addressing performance-related goals such as improved pelvic-spinal stabilization, deceleration of rotational movements, and improved propulsion for walking, sprinting, or jumping. Mastering this exercise should precede the Cable Trunk Rotation With Pull exercise presented in chapter 4.

Target Muscles

Posterior oblique subsystem (latissimus dorsi, contralateral gluteus maximus), teres major, posterior deltoids, scapular retractors, spinal extensors

Joint Motions

Scapular retraction, shoulder median extension, elbow flexion

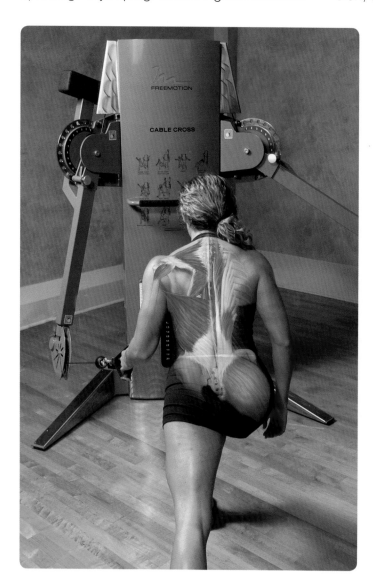

Cable One-Arm Low Lat Row

Alignment and Positioning

1. Grasp the handle, then step back from the pulley into a lunge position, with the opposite leg forward and the legs about shoulder-width apart.

2. Begin with the arm aligned with the cable, the scapula slightly protracted, and the weight mostly on the lead leg.

3. Position the spine in good posture, and draw a deep breath.

Motion and Stabilization

1. Begin to exhale, activate the core, and start to retract the shoulder blade while pulling the arm back and up.

2. Continue to retract the scapula, and pull the arm up and the hand toward the navel until the upper arm is about parallel to the body.

3. Hold, slowly inhale, and allow the arm and scapula to be pulled back to the starting position while maintaining proper posture.

Cable Overhead Lat Extension

This exercise targets the lats and associated shoulder extensors. This isolated shoulder movement is a good selection for some people to better develop initial facilitation of the lats as opposed to rowing or pulling movements. Depending on the active shoulder flexion abilities of the lifter, this exercise can allow for high degrees of resisted shoulder movement because the starting position can be drastically varied. The standing position requires additional hip, core, and trunk musculature for stabilization and makes the use of heavy weight difficult. One-arm, lunge positions, one-leg, alternate movements, and piston movements are optional variations for this exercise.

Target Muscles

Latissimus dorsi, teres major, posterior deltoids, scapular depressors and retractors, spinal extensors

Joint Motions

Scapular depression, scapular retraction, shoulder median extension

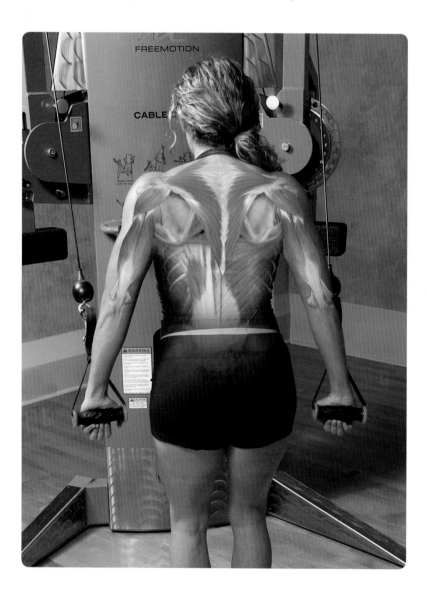

Cable Overhead Lat Extension

Alignment and Positioning

1. Hold the handles perpendicular to the body, then step back from the pulley with the legs about shoulder-width apart.

2. Begin with the hands just above the head, the arms straight, and the elbows slightly bent and pointed out.

3. Flex the hips and knees to position the trunk at about a 45-degree angle in good posture and with a natural arch in the lower spine. Draw a deep breath.

Motion and Stabilization

1. Begin to exhale, activate the core, and start to pull the shoulder blades down and together while pulling the arms down.

2. Continue to depress and retract the scapula, and pull the arms back as far as possible while maintaining proper posture.

3. Hold, slowly inhale, and allow the arms and scapula to be pulled back to the starting position while maintaining proper posture.

Machine Lat Pull-Up

Pulling exercises in the frontal plane require substantially more difficult scapular-thoracic and scapular-humeral rhythm than rowing exercises performed in the median plane require. This exercise still targets the lats but will also demand more from the rhomboids and other scapular downward rotators and scapular depressors. The ability to produce optimal posture, particularly in the thoracic spine, is a prerequisite for optimal frontal plane scapular movement. Frontal plane pulling with a bar forces a closed-chain action of the arms that can be stressful to the structures of the shoulder, elbow, and wrist joints.

Proper hand placement and technique are imperative in order to decrease these risks.

Target Muscles

Latissimus dorsi, teres major, posterior deltoids, scapular depressors, rhomboids, biceps

Joint Motions

Scapular depression, scapular downward rotation, shoulder frontal extension, elbow extension

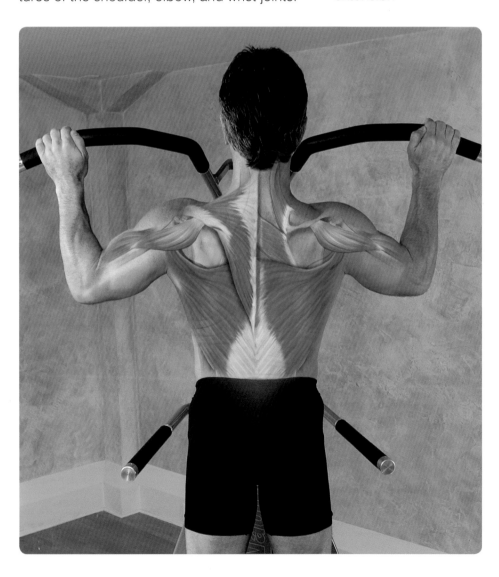

Alignment and Positioning

1. Grasp the bar with the hands outside shoulder width so that a 90-degree angle may be formed at the elbow as you pull up.

2. Begin with the knees on the pad if assistance is desired, with the arms straight, the elbows pointed out, and the scapula elevated.

3. Position the spine in good posture with the chest up, and draw a deep breath.

Motion and Stabilization

1. Begin to exhale, activate the core, and start to pull the shoulder blades down while pulling the elbows out and the body straight up between the hands.

2. Continue to depress and rotate the scapula downward. Pull the body up while keeping good posture and keeping the scapula depressed.

3. Hold, slowly inhale, and allow the body to lower and the scapula to return to the starting position while maintaining proper posture.

Cable One-Arm Lat Pull-Down

Pulling movements in the frontal plane require a more difficult scapular-thoracic and scapular-humeral rhythm than rowing movements that occur in the median plane require. This open-chain pulling movement allows for independent scapular and arm movement, which requires more scapular and shoulder control and can reduce some of the potentially destructive forces associated with closed-chain options. The one-arm movement while in a lunge position requires more assistance from the posterior oblique subsystem (POS) and other hip, core, and trunk muscles for stabilization than the seated, two-arm variations require. Lat pull-downs can also be per-formed with alternate or piston movements for varied training effects.

Target Muscles

Posterior oblique subsystem (latissimus dorsi, contralateral gluteus maximus), teres major, posterior deltoids, scapular depressors, rhomboids, biceps

Joint Motions

Scapular depression, scapular downward rotation, shoulder frontal extension, elbow flexion

Alignment and Positioning

1. Grasp the handle, then step back from the pulley into a lunge position, with the opposite leg forward and the legs about shoulder-width apart.

2. Begin with a natural arch in the lower spine, the arm straight, the elbow out, and the scapula rotated upward.

3. Position the trunk in good posture and in direct alignment with the cable. Slightly lift the chest up, and draw a deep breath.

Motion and Stabilization

1. Begin to exhale, activate the core, and start to pull the shoulder blade downward while keeping the elbow out as it flexes.

2. Continue to depress and rotate the scapula downward. Pull the arm down while keeping the hand away from the body and the upper arm and trunk in alignment with the cable.

3. Hold, slowly inhale, and allow the arm and scapula to be pulled out and up to the starting position while maintaining proper posture.

Dumbbell Shoulder Row

This exercise targets the posterior deltoids and also works the scapular retractors, shoulder external rotators, and biceps. In addition, the vertical pull of the resistance directly challenges the spinal erectors and hip extensors for trunk and pelvic stability. Although lifting free weights while standing has more transference to life situations, these types of exercises require a high level of hamstring flexibility in order to align the body properly against gravity. Using cable-pulley systems may be a better option for some people until appropriate hip mobility and spinal stability are achieved.

Target Muscles

Posterior deltoids, shoulder external rotators, scapular retractors, spinal extensors, hip extensors

Joint Motions

Scapular retraction, shoulder horizontal extension, elbow flexion

Dumbbell Shoulder Row

Alignment and Positioning

1. Hold the dumbbells with a neutral grip, and stand with the legs set outside shoulder width.

2. Flex the hips, slightly bend the knees, and lean the upper body over until the trunk is close to parallel with the floor. Maintain good posture and a natural arch in the lower spine.

3. Begin with the dumbbells perpendicular to the body, the hands straight down from the shoulders, and the spine in good posture. Draw a deep breath.

Motion and Stabilization

1. Begin to exhale, activate the core, and start to pull the shoulder blades together while pulling the arms out and up.

2. Continue to retract the scapula and maintain posture. Pull the arms out and up until the upper arms are about parallel to the floor, with the elbows straight out from the shoulders.

3. Hold, slowly inhale, and allow the arms and scapula to be pulled back to the starting position while maintaining proper posture.

Cable One-Arm Shoulder Row

This exercise targets the posterior deltoids but also works the scapular retractors, shoulder external rotators, and biceps. The one-arm, standing option has higher stabilization demands that will require more involvement of the posterior oblique subsystem (POS) and associated hip, core, and trunk muscles than the two-arm, seated options require. Exercises performed while standing may be more transferable to most life situations, but maximal loads are difficult because there is no use of an external anchor. For varied training effects, this exercise can be per- formed seated, kneeling, with two arms, or with alternate or piston arm movements.

Target Muscles

Posterior deltoids, shoulder external rotators, scapular retractors, spinal extensors, hip extensors, posterior oblique subsystem

Joint Motions

Scapular retraction, shoulder horizontal extension, elbow flexion

Alignment and Positioning

1. Grasp the handle, then step back from the pulley into a lunge position with the opposite leg forward and with the legs about shoulder-width apart.

2. Begin with the arm aligned with the cable, the elbow pointed out, the scapula slightly protracted, and the weight mostly over the lead leg.

3. Position the spine in good posture, and draw a deep breath.

Motion and Stabilization

1. Begin to exhale, activate the core, and start to retract the shoulder blade while pulling the arm out and back.

2. Continue to retract the scapula and maintain posture. Pull the arm out and back until the elbow is about parallel to the shoulder, keeping the upper arm parallel to the floor.

3. Hold, slowly inhale, and allow the arm and scapula to be pulled back to the starting position while maintaining proper posture.

Barbell Scapular Elevation (Shrug)

This exercise targets the scapula elevators and upper back and neck extensors. This exercise could have been included in pushing movements as well, because the trapezius (one of the targeted muscles) is primarily responsible for upward rotation of the scapula, which is necessary for overhead pushing movements. The technique presented for this exercise contains important modifications to the traditional "shrug" movement and can help to prepare scapular and upper spinal muscles for power training exercises, such as the modified clean or hang clean. Notice that the trunk is positioned in a forward lean at the hips. This alignment allows for greater trapezius and scapular retractor involvement, which consequently helps to decrease the load on the levator scapula muscles and reduce stress on the cervical spine.

Target Muscles

Upper and mid trapezius, levator scapula, cervical and upper spinal extensors

Joint Motions

Scapular elevation and retraction

Barbell Scapular Elevation (Shrug)

Alignment and Positioning

1. Stand in good posture with the feet directly under the hips. Grasp the bar using an overhand grip, with the hands just outside shoulder width.

2. Draw a deep breath, flex the hips and knees slightly, and begin to push the hips back and lean the trunk forward.

3. Position the spine at an approximate 45-degree angle, with good posture and a natural arch in the lower spine, and with the bar close to the thighs.

Motion and Stabilization

1. Begin to exhale, activate the core, and start to pull the shoulder blades up and together while keeping the arms relaxed.

2. Continue to elevate and retract the scapula, lifting the arms and weight while pushing the chest out to improve posture.

3. Hold, then slowly inhale and allow the arms and scapula to be pulled back to the starting position while maintaining posture.

Cable Shoulder External Rotation

This exercise targets the posterior rotator cuff muscles. A similar exercise that trains internal rotation of the shoulder could be performed to target the subscapularis. Although strengthening the entire rotator cuff musculature would be advised, it is the external rotators that tend to become weak with faulty postural adaptations and are also more prone to injury. This is because the external rotators have less support from larger muscles than the internal rotators do. The external rotators are also required for deceleration of the arm during any throwing or swinging movements, leaving them at high risk for injury. Strong rotator cuff muscles should be considered a prerequisite for ballistic exercises such as cleans or snatches.

Target Muscles

Infraspinatus, teres minor

Joint Motions

Shoulder external rotation

Alignment and Positioning

1. Stand in good posture, and set the adjustable pulley at elbow height with a single-handle attachment.

2. Place a rolled towel under the elbow to abduct the upper arm about 10 to 20 degrees, and flex the elbow to 90 degrees.

3. Begin with the arm internally rotated. Stabilize the scapula and draw a deep breath.

Motion and Stabilization

1. Begin to exhale, activate the core, and start to rotate the shoulder, pulling the arm out and across the body and keeping the elbow fixed.

2. Continue to pull the arm out, keeping the wrist neutral and the elbow pressed against the towel. Maintain good posture and a stable scapula.

3. Hold, slowly inhale, and allow the arm to be pulled back to the starting position while maintaining elbow, scapular, and postural positioning.

Dumbbell Horizontal Plane Shoulder External Rotation

This exercise targets combined strengthening of the shoulder abductors and posterior rotator cuff muscles. The arm is positioned slightly below 90 degrees of abduction. This position better targets different fibers of the infraspinatus, provides a stabilization demand for the deltoid muscles, and allows for full external rotation with less chance of impingement than when in higher positions of shoulder abduction. The elbow is held at 90 degrees, and an isolated movement is performed to ensure specific targeting of the external rotators. Working in a standing position and using free weights make this exercise more transferable to life situations. Strengthening the rotator cuff should be considered a prerequisite for ballistic movements such as cleans or snatches.

Target Muscles

Infraspinatus, teres minor, deltoids, scapular stabilizers

Joint Motions

Shoulder external rotation

Dumbbell Horizontal Plane Shoulder External Rotation

Alignment and Positioning

1. Stand in good posture, with the hips and knees slightly flexed and the trunk in a forward lean.

2. Abduct the arms to about 80 degrees, with the elbows bent at 90 degrees, keeping the wrists neutral. Position the lower arms and the dumbbells about parallel to the floor.

3. Stabilize the spine and shoulders, then draw a deep breath.

Motion and Stabilization

1. Begin to exhale, activate the core, and start to rotate the shoulders, pulling the lower arms and the dumbbells up while keeping the wrists straight.

2. Continue to rotate the shoulders and pull the arms up as far as possible, keeping the forward lean of the trunk with the spine in good posture and the upper arms at about 80 degrees.

3. Hold, then slowly inhale, and allow the arms and dumbbells to lower to the starting position while maintaining posture and shoulder positioning.

Dumbbell Biceps Flexion With Supination

This exercise targets the full action of the elbow flexors. Although isolated elbow flexion is often selected for aesthetic-based goals, the technique presented here requires significant levels of stabilization demand for scapular depressors and retractors, so it may help improve postural abilities as well as develop the biceps. The offset position of the dumbbells further challenges supination, and the slight initial shoulder flexion helps to promote scapular actions that are associated with good posture. Variations of this exercise include maintaining the elbows in a neutral position to target the brachioradialis, or in supinated positions to better target the biceps brachii.

Target Muscles

Biceps group, wrist flexors, shoulder and scapular stabilizers

Joint Motions

Elbow flexion, radioulnar supination

Dumbbell Biceps Flexion With Supination

Alignment and Positioning

1. Stand with the hips and knees slightly flexed, and hold a set of dumbbells, with the lower arms in a neutral position.

2. Slightly retract the shoulder blades, and position the spine in good posture. Slide the hands all the way forward on the handles of the dumbbells to unbalance the load.

3. Begin with the hands and dumbbells straight down from the shoulders, with the elbows slightly bent. Draw a deep breath.

Motion and Stabilization

1. Begin to exhale, activate the core, and slightly flex the shoulders to begin pulling the arms forward while also flexing the elbows.

2. Continue to flex the elbows, and begin supinating the lower arms, causing the dumbbells to twist as they are pulled forward and up as far as possible. Maintain scapular and trunk positioning.

3. Hold, then slowly inhale and allow the arms to slowly lower and twist back to the starting position while maintaining proper posture.

Cable One-Arm 90-Degree Biceps Flexion

This exercise targets the biceps group. It emphasizes the short head of the biceps by preshortening the long-head biceps, which causes it to become somewhat active insufficient. The shoulder positioning used in this exercise also creates different scapular and shoulder stabilization demands than lower angles. If using a barbell as opposed to separate handles, it is important to grasp the bar with the natural carrying angle in place to decrease some of the additional shearing forces associated with most closed-chain upper body exercises. Individual handles also allow two-hand, alternate, and piston movements for varied training effects.

Target Muscles

Biceps group, wrist flexors, shoulder and scapular stabilizers

Joint Motions

Elbow flexion, radioulnar supination

Cable One-Arm 90-Degree Biceps Flexion

Alignment and Positioning

1. Stand with the hips and knees slightly flexed, and grasp the handle of the upper cable in a supinated position.

2. Pull the shoulder blades slightly together, slightly lift the chest, and position the spine in good posture.

3. Position the arm in line with the cable pulley, and begin with tension on the biceps. Draw a deep breath.

Motion and Stabilization

1. Begin to exhale, activate the core, slightly flex the shoulder, and begin to pull the arm up while flexing the elbow.

2. Continue to pull the lower arm up and back as far as possible while maintaining scapular, shoulder, wrist, and postural positioning.

3. Hold, then slowly inhale and allow the arm to be slowly pulled back to the starting position while maintaining proper posture.

Program Design

What makes up a resistance exercise program? If you ask almost any fitness enthusiast or even most fitness professionals this question, you will probably get a similar response. A resistance training program is typically viewed as simply a collection of selected exercises grouped together for the purpose of accomplishing a person's goals. Although this sounds like a logical answer, it is actually a definition of a routine rather than a program. It is this same simplistic approach to programming that often leads to only minimal progress, failure to reach a person's goals, and programs that often completely ignore the person's needs. This chapter, though only a brief summary of all that could be presented on this topic, should help you understand the primary concepts involved in resistance exercise programming and help you develop the thought process needed to design better programs. Programming is a science, but it is also an art to those who practice and provide fitness programs professionally. By becoming well acquainted with the information provided in this chapter, you should also be able to better separate good advice from poor in relation to accomplishing your own personal goals and addressing your specific individual needs.

Routines Versus Programs

According to the dictionary definitions, there are differences between a routine and a program, yet in fitness, these terms are often used interchangeably. Let's look at the definitions of these two words derived from an unbiased linguistic view before we discuss the meanings and differences from a fitness perspective.

Routine—A ritual; a series of actions or behaviors performed on a regular basis; to repetitively practice a normal or regular way of doing things.

This is exactly how many people approach their fitness programs and precisely why their progress is limited. To believe that continued progress can be achieved by simply performing a collection of movement patterns on a repetitive or routine basis would be contrary to all we have come to know about the human body. We know that muscles have the ability to adapt to certain stimuli. But without progressive stimuli, there cannot be progressive adaptation. As briefly presented in chapter 1, all exercises are specific movement patterns that provide only a limited and specific set of stimuli. Once that set of stimuli has been learned and adapted to, not much more information can be obtained until the movement has been modified in some manner. Basically, this means that without new input, no new adaptations will likely be made, which is not an efficient plan for anyone looking for progression as opposed to maintenance.

Program—A specific system of instructions; to provide a detailed set of instructions for achieving a specific purpose; a purposeful plan of action.

These definitions most often relate programs to how they would be used by a computer. In chapter 1, we discussed how many experts on motor learning compared the control-sensorimotor system to a very advanced computer system. The control system processes the stimuli produced by any exercise movement, compares the information to original instructions, attempts to perfect the movement, then stores the movement for future recall—all while the active and passive systems are physiologically adapting to the demands of the exercise in order to develop muscles and joints that exhibit improved biomotor abilities, such as strength, endurance, mobility, stability, speed, power, or agility. As a by-product of these processes, muscles may hypertrophy and body fat reduction may occur that will alter the composition of the body. For many people, these aesthetic adaptations and changes in one's appearance are the primary driving force behind exercising in the first place, but these changes are dependent on the proper stimuli being provided by the program.

Therefore, from these technical descriptions of routines and programs, we can further derive general definitions for fitness or resistance training routines and programs as follows:

A routine—A collection of carefully selected exercise movements performed with specific techniques for a specified period of time.

A program—An organized series of routines that are systematically varied in a purposeful and specific manner in order to achieve periodic goals and address identified needs.

The primary focus of *Muscle Mechanics* is to teach safe and efficient resistance training technique. However, you also need to learn how to select resistance training exercises, group them into realistic yet challenging routines, and then organize and vary the routines to design short-, mid-, and long-term or periodic programs. The rest of this chapter is dedicated to providing the information needed to help you develop the thought process for doing this.

Resistance Training Exercise Variables

This section picks up on the topic discussed in chapter 2, "Effective Exercise Selection." In that chapter, information was presented on how to select exercises that coincide with the person's goals or needs, produce the appropriate movement pattern, target the desired muscle groups, and offer superior neuromuscular benefits compared to the musculoskeletal risks.

Once an exercise movement has been selected, there are many choices for varying that exercise. Think of the almost infinite number of ways you could vary any resistance exercise, such as the specific technique that is used, how much resistance is applied, how much and how often the exercise is performed, what order the exercises are arranged in, and how much rest is planned between exercises. A well-designed program will help dictate how all exercise variables should be selected. A periodized program will have planned cycles broken down into set phases that will determine how each variable of every exercise should be manipulated.

Resistance training exercise variables may be grouped into five general categories as follows:

1. Technique

2. Intensity

3. Volume

4. Recovery

5. Sequence

As stated, teaching proper exercise technique is the primary mission of this book. The previous chapters have already provided a substantial amount of information pertaining to what constitutes efficient and safe technique and how it affects the structure and performance abilities of the human body. Therefore, this chapter won't cover these concepts again, other than to reiterate that technique is always an option or variable that should be carefully considered before beginning an exercise. In my opinion, technique is the most important variable for any resistance training exercise and will largely determine the success or failure of the program.

Intensity

Intensity is often presented as the most important variable a person can manipulate for any exercise. Many people argue that it surpasses even technique because the intensity, or amount of resistance, will affect technique. Though this sounds reasonable, my view is that any time the intensity forces a change in alignment, positioning, motion, stabilization, tempo, or even breathing, it is probably too high. However, intensity is an extremely important variable to consider, control, and alter when necessary because it will affect all other variables either directly or indirectly. Intensity also relates directly to the body's adaptation ability and the *principle of progressive overload*. This principle states that sufficient intensity and duration must be applied to overload the muscle's present levels of adaptation in order to improve strength or endurance.

Intensity can generally be defined as the level of effort produced as compared to the maximal effort possible. In resistance training, intensity is usually related to the load or amount of resistance used. Intensity loads are often expressed as a percentage of a one-repetition maximum effort (or percent of 1RM). For example, if a person was performing repetitions of an exercise with 70 percent of what the person could maximally lift on a single attempt, this would be classified as 70 percent of 1RM. Actually testing a person's maximal effort for a single repetition on any exercise would be high risk, to say the least, so it is not practical or necessary for most individuals. However, close estimates can be made from completion of submaximal tests.

One popular system estimates that the amount of resistance adequate for a six-repetition maximum would equal approximately 85 percent of a person's one-repetition maximum. In practice, however, I have found this number to vary significantly from person to person and from exercise to exercise. I have also concluded that for most people, there is no need and little value in determining what their single-repetition maximum is, whether actual or estimated. In fact, since intensity and volume have an interdependent relationship, intensity will only be described and derived in this book as it relates to the prescribed volume.

For example, in the sample routines provided later in this chapter, no intensity is cited for any exercise. Instead, a recommended range of repetitions with a recommended tempo is given for each exercise (each exercise is also expected to be performed with the other specific elements of technique presented in this book). Each person is responsible for finding the appropriate weight that he or she can use to complete the given volume and perform with the proper techniques. This will take some trial and error to find, and it will also need to be adjusted as the recommended repetitions, tempo, or any other element of technique is changed.

When selecting a weight load for a new exercise, always start with low levels of resistance to first practice the technique and learn the movement pattern. Then progress the intensity to better match your repetition goals for the given phase of training. Be sure to also decrease the intensity when needed as you fatigue and can no longer complete the repetition goal with proper technique.

Intensity and Volume Relationships

Intensity's relationship to volume is probably the most critical to understand because there are so many components of volume. Overall, most experts agree that there are strong reasons to decrease total volume as intensity increases. The major difference of opinion among experts is in how much volume should be decreased, and in what manner it should be done. Volume consists of more than just the number of repetitions and the tempo or speed in which they are performed. The number of sets in a given routine, and the duration and frequency of the routines themselves, also need to be considered. The following sections summarize how intensity relates to each component of volume.

Intensity and Repetitions   One component of volume that is relatively easy to adjust in relation to changes in intensity is the number of repetitions performed. This relationship is automatically regulated by the person's present neuromuscular abilities. As intensity increases, the repetitions naturally decrease, leading toward the desired objective of decreased total volume. The opposite is also true—if intensity is decreased, then more repetitions are possible, which may result in increases in total volume. This automated relationship of intensity to repetitions should be acknowledged but should not dictate actual increases or decreases in total volume. This decision should be predetermined by the program and accounted for in the assignment of all other components of volume for each phase of each cycle. Intensity-to-volume relationships can easily be controlled with even minimal amounts of planning, because every other component of volume is a choice that is not directly determined by the intensity.

Intensity and Tempo   Intensity should influence tempo as well. The natural effect of greater resistance is that it will move faster as it is lowered and move slower as it is raised because heavier loads are more difficult to decelerate and accelerate. However, tempo can have a dramatic effect on the specific type of strength adaptations that are achieved. Therefore, assignment of specific repetition speeds should be predetermined by the program rather than dictated by the intensity loads. This being said, intensity will influence tempo, particularly as intensity levels are increased. Since it is proportionally more difficult to control heavier loads, tempo should generally be reduced when intensity is increased. This recommendation does not apply to power-related movements, such as cleans or snatches, for which technique is reliant on higher speeds of movement. Be cautious, however, because as physics and common sense both point out, moving heavier loads faster will always increase potential risk.

Intensity and Sets   The number of sets performed is always a choice (and one that is sometimes given little thought). There is a well-established, yet rarely applied, training principle that addresses this issue. This principle simply states that as intensity increases and repetitions decrease, the number of sets should be increased. This is particularly true for anyone who desires even minor amounts of muscle growth or hypertrophy. Muscle hypertrophy is the increase in muscle size that accompanies tissue adaptations to stress created from the combination of intensity and volume of resistance training. Smaller amounts of muscle hypertrophy give people the muscle "tone" or definition they often desire, while larger amounts of hypertrophy develop the muscle "mass" that others may desire. In either case, the combination of intensity and volume is critical for any hypertrophy to occur. If sets are not added to offset the reduction of repetitions in response to higher intensity loads, the resulting decrease in total volume often makes it difficult to gain or even maintain muscle hypertrophy.

Intensity, Duration, and Frequency   Intensity should also have an indirect effect on the duration and frequency of any routine. Duration and frequency have an inverse relationship. The duration of a routine is determined by the total volume performed in that session, and the frequency of routines is related directly to their duration. More recovery time is typically recommended as duration increases, so this would mean a decrease in frequency. Therefore, if sets are to be increased as intensity is increased for each exercise in a given routine, then duration would be naturally increased and frequency decreased. This may not be a wise choice because most people are limited in their options for how long and how often they can exercise. I have found it unproductive to make any dramatic alterations to the actual frequency or duration of a person's exercise schedule. Therefore, another component of volume needs to be considered, and that is the number of exercises performed in a given routine.

Since any exercise, whether intentionally or unintentionally, emphasizes certain muscle groups and neglects others, most exercises can be classified by the muscles they target. Therefore, the total amount of exercises selected per body part in a given routine should be considered when making intensity and volume adjustments. When increasing intensity, decreasing reps, adding sets, and using slower tempos, it is also logical to reduce the number of exercises per body part. This not only maintains proper ratios of volume and intensity but also provides for the extra recovery needed when working with heavier loads. It can also allow for adherence to preplanned duration and frequency schedules.

It should be clear that there is much to consider when attempting to continually determine the changes in volume that should accompany changes in intensity. People who carry on routines for too long with volume-to-intensity relationships that are too high can experience overtraining, fatigue, decreases in performance, impaired health, and increased risk of injury. Conversely, routines that contain volume-to-intensity relationships that are too low not only lack sufficient work for muscle hypertrophy, but they also probably won't provide enough stimulation for the neural adaptations necessary for significant improvements in strength; these routines also may not elicit the beneficial hormonal responses conducive to gains in muscle and increased metabolic activity. Table 9.1 depicts all the various relationships discussed in this section and the changes in each component of volume in relation to increases in intensity. This concise and easy-to-follow chart should help you better understand these relationships so you can design more effective resistance training programs.

Intensity and Recovery

When intensity is increased, it not only stresses the joints and tissues of the passive and active systems, but it also stresses the neural structures of the control system. It is well documented that nerve cells take five or six times as long to recover as muscle cells do. In certain high-intensity training phases, recommended rest intervals of up to five to eight minutes between sets are not uncommon. This allows for nearly complete neural recovery as well as metabolic recovery. As seen in table 9.1, more planned recovery should be allowed for when using higher intensity loads. However, rest periods between sets do not need to be absolute in most phases of training. Often an "active recovery," such as performing supersets with movement patterns that are opposite or unrelated to the previous movement, is an option for completing rest. This still allows for adequate recovery of the specific motor units previously recruited, and it also supplies more opportunity for increased overall work. This is a logical choice in certain phases because usually other exercises and training goals must also be accomplished during the session.

TABLE 9.1 Volume and Intensity Relationships

Training goals	Intensity	Repetitions	Sets	Subtotal 1	Tempo assignment	Subtotal 2	Exercise/ muscle group	Initial volume	Rest between sets
Endurance	X	17	2	34 reps	2111 (5 sec)	170 sec	3	520 sec	30-60 sec
Hypertrophy	X+Y	10	3	30 reps	3121 (7 sec)	210 sec	2	420 sec	60-240 sec
Strength	X+Y+Z	5	5	25 reps	4122 (9 sec)	225 sec	1	225 sec	300+ sec

Intensity and Sequence

The intensity level of an exercise will also dictate its preferred placement in the sequence of the routine. The higher the intensity level, the more the neural demand, so the earlier in the routine it would logically be placed. However, certain biomechanical factors—such as the exercise's effect on stabilizers needed for subsequent movements, or the priority of overall goals—may occasionally cause a change to this sequencing guideline. It is also reasonable to purposely spread intense exercises throughout the routine rather than place them all at the beginning. This would require a more consistent level of effort throughout the routine and would probably promote a more consistent hormonal response as well. This type of sequence would be preferred for most people as compared to routines that quickly elevate lactic acid and hormonal response and then allow them to plummet as the workout wanes. In any case, always keep in mind that the later a high-intensity exercise is placed in the sequence of a routine, the worse the performance is likely to be.

Volume

Volume for a muscle is the total amount of time it is under tension. This can be broken down into *initial volume,* which is the total amount of time under tension for a given muscle during a single routine, and total volume. Initial volume is originally calculated by multiplying the number of repetitions by the number of sets, and then by the tempo of each rep. Each movement that targets that area would also need to be considered for determining initial volume. *Total volume* can be further described in weekly, monthly, or yearly periods. Total volume can also be calculated for a given phase, mesocycle, or macrocycle simply by multiplying the initial volume of a routine by the frequency it was performed during the phase or cycle desired. Tracking volume is a simple matter of disciplined record keeping, which is more easily accomplished if the amounts of desired volume for each muscle group during each routine were previously planned and directed by the program. This preplanning and calculation ensures that proper volumes are obtained by simply following the workouts already drawn up beforehand.

Repetitions

Probably the most critical component of volume is the number of repetitions performed. As previously stated, the desired number of repetitions should be used to select the intensity, as opposed to the opposite scenario. The repetitions combined with the prescribed tempo will also dictate the duration of any set, which determines the energy systems and muscle fiber types that will be trained and the neural-metabolic adaptations a person can expect from that set. More metabolic adaptations necessary for muscular endurance occur when muscles are trained with lighter intensities and for longer durations of time under tension. Greater neural and intramuscular adaptations are experienced with sets performed at higher intensities and with shorter times under tension.

Low-repetition sets with higher intensities also require more use of the short-term energy system or ATP-CP (adenosine triphosphate-creatine phosphate). This combination would also recruit more type IIB muscle fibers, which would be more appropriate for strength and power goals. Conversely, high-repetition sets performed with lighter loads work more into the aerobic or oxidative energy system and require more activation of type IIC and type I muscle fibers. These muscle fibers and this energy system are ideal for use in activities requiring greater amounts of muscular endurance. Moderate-repetition sets with moderate-intensity loads require more contributions from the glycolytic or lactic acid energy systems and target the various type IIA fibers.

This mid zone provides the stimulus for a blend of strength and endurance adaptations and is also associated with the greatest increases in muscle hypertrophy. This is why many resources recommend and most people tend to gravitate to a constant mid-range repetition and intensity combination for their resistance training routines. Though this sounds like good advice, research, most experts, and practical experience point to the fact that people who use a program that periodically varies the repetitions and intensity (along with all other components of volume) by far make greater gains than those who consistently train in the same zone, which can only provide the same repetitive stimulus. Table 9.2 depicts the correlation of time under tension with the energy systems, muscle fiber types, and neural-metabolic adaptations.

By using this chart, the proper duration of any set for the desired training goals can be accomplished simply by selecting the amount of resistance required to be challenged during the listed time under tension. Estimates of the number of repetitions performed that correspond to the targeted amount of time under tension are also given. When using these numbers, however, it is assumed that an average tempo of six seconds per repetition is used. More or fewer reps can be produced in the same amount of time under tension by adjusting the tempo, but this should cause little change in metabolic or neural adaptations. However, different tempos may elicit different types of specific strength adaptations, which will be discussed next.

Tempo

Tempo is described as the specific speed of a given repetition. Tempo has a much more dramatic training effect than simply its contribution to volume. Tempo is also a part of technique and can have a definitive influence on the specific type of strength that will be developed. Intrafusal muscle fibers, or muscle spindles, are sensitive to the speed of muscle contraction. They relay detailed information pertaining to changes in the length and tension of the muscles to the appropriate level of the control system for processing. Once information on speed of contraction, speed of force production, and rate of acceleration is learned and stored in the control system, specific intramuscular adaptations can then be recalled and used for similar demands in appropriate situations. As presented in chapter 3, I prefer to assign tempo using a four-digit number that represents the number of seconds for each phase and therefore dictates the precise movement speed throughout the repetition. The first number represents the eccentric phase, the second the eccentric-isometric phase, the third the concentric phase, and the fourth the concentric-isometric phase.

Certain tempos are more suited for achieving specific types of strength gains, such as maximal strength, static strength, explosive strength, and starting or acceleration strength needed

TABLE 9.2   Neural-Metabolic Continuum of Adaptation

Energy system (continuum)	Primary muscle fiber types stimulated	Time under tension	Neural-metabolic adaptation (continuum)	Specific training goals	Suggested recovery between sets
ATP-CP	IIB	1-10 secs (1-2 reps)*	Neural adaptation	Strength/power	5+ min
	IIaB IIAB IIAb			Strength-hypertrophy	
Glycolytic/lactic acid	IIA	30-90 secs (6-15 reps)*		Hypertrophy	1-4 min
	IIAC IIC			Hypertrophy-endurance	
	IC I	180+ secs (30+ reps)*	Metabolic adaptations	Endurance	0-30 secs
Oxidative/aerobic					

*Average tempo of 6 seconds

for improved speed. For example, stability strength would benefit from slow, controlled tempos with pauses at critical points of the movement to help develop stronger joint stability, such as a 2421 tempo. Gains in starting speed strength would require a tempo with pauses at the eccentric-isometric phase combined with a fast concentric phase of the repetition to teach the muscle to contract quickly from a set prelengthened position, such as a 2211 tempo. On the other hand, explosive strength would benefit most from a tempo that assigns a quick eccentric movement immediately followed by a quick concentric movement, with no pause in between in order to use the stretch reflex to increase power, such as a 1011 tempo. For general strength and hypertrophy goals, a controlled eccentric and concentric phase with slight pauses at the changeover points, such as a 2121 or a 3120, is recommended.

Sets

The number of sets performed is always an option, regardless of intensity levels or repetitions, with contemporary literature providing recommendations ranging from 1 to 12 sets depending on the goals. As previously discussed, there should typically be an inverse relationship between the number of sets and the number of repetitions performed, and a correlating relationship of sets with changes in intensity. This principle of increasing sets proportionally with intensity increases in order to maintain a certain level of overall volume can be altered for special cases when increased strength is needed along with a maintenance or decrease in muscle size. Think about a wrestler or a figure skater or many women who wish to get stronger but have no desire for increased muscle size. For these individuals, working with heavier loads and allowing the volume to decrease at a steeper rate may make sense. However, large and often even moderate amounts of muscle hypertrophy are not as easy to achieve as some people fear and most likely will not happen by accident.

Overall body mass, muscle size, muscle type, gender, and present level of conditioning all influence the number of sets prescribed as well. Larger people tend to receive greater benefits from more sets than smaller individuals do, if conditioning is appropriate. Larger muscles typically respond better to more sets than smaller muscles. Fast-twitch muscles develop better with more sets and heavier loads, while slow-twitch muscles respond more to fewer sets with lighter loads. The average male responds better to more sets than the average female does. More-experienced and better-conditioned individuals will tolerate and often need more sets and overall volume to experience progress. Conversely, beginners cannot recover from higher volumes of training and can often benefit from as little as one set. The key for these individuals should be the quality of the sets rather than the quantity.

Duration

Duration is another component of volume that should be well planned when designing resistance exercise programs. *Duration* is a general term that could be used to describe about any portion of volume, such as the duration of a single repetition or set, the duration of a routine or session, and the duration of a phase, cycle, or overall program. The duration of a repetition is the total tempo time and should be determined by the specific type of strength gains desired. Duration of a set is based on the neural-metabolic adaptations needed to achieve the strength, hypertrophy, or endurance goals. The duration of a routine is based primarily on the total number of sets and the amount of recovery given between each set. This can vary and may be determined by the person's present condition or the time the person has available for training. Recommended duration of a routine or single session of resistance training is typically from 30 to 60 minutes, because the normal level of glycogen stores will likely be almost drained by this time. The duration of phases, cycles, and programs depends totally on the overall program design. More information on these topics will be provided later in this chapter.

Frequency

Frequency, like duration, is a general term that for our purposes relates to how often an exercise, a routine, a phase, or a cycle is performed. The frequency of any exercise is dependent on several factors, such as the newness of the exercise, its complexity, or its deemed importance for addressing needs or accomplishing goals. An exercise must be performed often enough, particularly when new or of high complexity, in order to develop and store the various and specific stimuli of the new or modified motor program. Too often, people do not initially perform a new exercise using proper technique with enough frequency, resulting in storing faulty motor patterns that are inefficient and involve compensation. On the other hand, too high a frequency of the same exercises with exclusion of others can create *pattern overload,* which may result in development of muscular imbalances, connective tissue strain, and possible increased wear of joint surfaces.

Frequency of a routine depends on several factors, one of which is recovery. Frequency of routines can also be set by the training phase, cycle, or the overall program design, which means that frequency may vary throughout the year. However, all of this being considered, I have found that frequency of routines is most often determined by the person's schedule and time allotment for exercise as opposed to scientific reasons. Most people must start with how much frequency they can realistically adhere to, and then design the program around these limits. Therefore, routines should usually be designed with only minor changes of frequency throughout any phase, cycle, or overall program so that individuals can adhere to their regular schedules of training.

Recovery

Recovery is an essential variable for performance of a set or the entire routine. Recovery is influenced by intensity and should be closely correlated with initial and overall volume. Recovery is necessary for the adaptation process, and tissue repair may take 2 to 10 days following a single session depending on the individual, the levels of intensity and volume, and the muscle's physiological makeup. All muscles recover at different rates, with larger ones taking longer than smaller ones and fast-twitch muscles taking longer than slow-twitch muscles. Larger people may also take longer to recover than smaller people, depending on present condition, experience with training, and genetics. Therefore, exercise routines for large people that include high-intensity, low-rep training that targets larger fast-twitch muscles will probably need more recovery and less frequency than smaller people performing low-intensity, high-rep training that targets smaller slow-twitch muscles. You should always remember that muscles only become stronger, bigger, or develop more stamina on the days they are resting, not when training.

Lack of recovery between workout routines leads to exhaustion and overtraining. *Exhaustion* is the result of short-term imbalances of stress and recovery, whereas *overtraining* is the long-term result. Overtraining causes declines in tissue repair and nervous system function. It can create hormonal imbalances and often results in severe deficiencies of the immune system, leaving the person weaker, chronically fatigued, mentally drained, and prone to illness and injury. Here is where self-awareness, instinct, and common sense must be applied along with the science of program design. At times, the body simply cannot keep pace with even the best-planned training programs. This is often due to uncontrollable variables in a person's life that gradually or suddenly add more stress to the equation than was anticipated. When life changes such as personal issues, job stress, or illness arise, more recovery becomes necessary, and duration of routines and perhaps frequency of routines may need to be adjusted.

The amount of recovery between sets should be planned and adhered to as much as possible. The rest periods between sets are as important as the stimulus itself for achieving the neural-metabolic adaptations desired (see table 9.2). As previously stated, more rest is needed when working with higher intensity sets, which require greater neural drive, than when performing sets with lower intensity, which depend more on metabolic factors for recovery.

If full recovery between sets is not required for goal achievement, then muscles can often recover adequately enough through "active rest," such as by performing supersets or active stretching for muscle groups opposing or unrelated to the ones being targeted. These "active rest" periods may be an extremely valuable use of training time. They may allow the individual to continue to progress toward other training goals or needs, such as increasing mobility, targeting stabilizers or weak links, or simply increasing overall volume for metabolic and hypertrophy purposes.

Sequence

Sequence may be defined as the specific planned exercise order in a given routine. It is the program variable that must allow for the largest amount of random change in a training program. This is due to the numerous uncontrollable variables that can influence exercise sequence. For example, having less time than planned for the training session, training at a different facility with different equipment, broken equipment, a recent strain or injury, or simply having to work around other people are just a few of the situations that can force a change of the routine and interrupt the planned exercise sequence.

Any time an exercise is moved from its originally designed sequence, it will be affected and will also affect all following exercises to some degree. For example, imagine if the Barbell Squat exercise was planned for the first circuit but was not available until much later in the routine after other leg and back work had been performed. Those exercises would probably seem easier, while obviously the intensity and perhaps even the volume of the Barbell Squat would probably need to be altered. However, changes in volume should be kept within the planned training parameters to continue to pursue the proper neural-metabolic adaptations desired in the present phase of the program cycle.

Numerous guidelines have been given in literature and applied in practice that may be helpful for designing efficient sequencing of exercise routines. Keep in mind these are only guidelines and not rules. Experienced and advanced individuals with higher levels of neuromuscular efficiency can purposely go outside most guidelines to accomplish different training effects. There are valid reasons for ignoring any guideline for the right person and for the proper goal.

Here are the five guidelines I have found to be the most helpful:

1. Place exercises of high neurological challenge and demand (such as those with greater stability and balance demand) before those of low demand.

2. Place high-priority exercises before those of lower priority, such as training general movement pattern exercises before isolated movements.

3. Place new exercises with higher motor learning requirements before ones previously mastered or with low motor learning requirements.

4. Place high-intensity exercises before those of lower intensity, and place those planned for application of heavy loads and multiple sets before supplemental exercises.

5. Place exercises targeting stabilizers (such as rotator cuff, ankle supinator, and specific core work) at the end of the routine.

Periodization and Program Design

The key to designing effective short-, mid-, and long-term resistance exercise programs is to develop a system that efficiently plans, organizes, and manages all exercise variables. *Periodization* can be defined as a system for program design that plans appropriate cycles and phases, organizes routines, and systematically manipulates all acute exercise variables. Theories and definitions of periodization vary widely, but the basic concepts are time proven for success and have been used by trainers and strength coaches since the early 1950s. The origin of periodization is credited to professionals in Russia and other Eastern Bloc countries, and it was later adopted by those in the United States who had witnessed the superior performances of other countries' athletes in world competition.

Research has confirmed periodization's ability to produce significantly better results than straight set training or linear progression models. A continual variety of training stimuli is definitely needed in order to progress after initial adaptations have taken place. The neuromuscular system strives for efficiency and adapts as quickly as possible to new stimuli, but only to a certain extent before progression halts or even reverses. The previous information in this chapter alone should confirm that maintaining the optimal relationships between all exercise variables is not possible without a programming system in place. Since resistance exercise selection and methods of systematically manipulating resistance exercise variables have already been presented, the most important things left to cover are how to plan program cycles and organize training phases in ways that will make the overall program effective in accomplishing goals and addressing needs.

Program Cycles

A resistance exercise program should be considered as always ongoing but should be broken down into long- and short-term blocks or periods of time that can be termed "cycles." Breaking a program down into cycles is helpful for prioritizing training goals and needs. Cycles can vary greatly in the amount of time they span. They are designed to apply more focus on certain goals and needs while placing less attention on others based on established priorities. Macrocycles are long-term cycles that may encompass several months to a year and help to set the priorities and time lines in which to accomplish training goals or address individual needs. Macrocycles will need to be further broken down into more manageable segments called "mesocycles."

Mesocycles enable a person to better track progress, reassess goals and needs, design new routines, and make any needed adjustments (to training, diet, sleep, and so on) in order to stay on the time lines set forth by the macrocycle. Mesocycles can also vary widely in length, usually ranging from 3 to 12 weeks. I have found that 6- to 8-week mesocycles work well for most people. This is enough time to experience significant and measurable results, yet not become bored with the present routines. This time frame is also short enough to allow a person to identify and correct controllable problems and adjust for uncontrollable variables that may have surfaced before they can inhibit further progress. People should reassess and gather as much pertinent data as possible between mesocycles to help design the new routines appropriately for continued success.

Training Phases

Mesocycles are planned to focus on certain priorities, but all other goals or needs should not be completely ignored in the process. Other than competitive athletes who may only need to focus on a specific set of biomotor abilities (such as strength, endurance, or speed), most people desire and could benefit from improvements in several if not all of these areas. Therefore, if a person spends a 6- to 8-week mesocycle completely striving for strength, that person may lose endurance or mobility if these biomotor abilities are not also reinforced to some degree. Balancing priorities within a mesocycle is exactly what training phases are designed to do.

Many experts believe that it is ineffective to attempt to improve on every biomotor ability simultaneously during each training routine, because there is not enough time in a 30- to 60-minute session to adequately apply and adapt to that much varied stimuli. Therefore, a mesocycle can be divided into training phases lasting 1 to 3 weeks that focus primarily on only certain neuro-metabolic adaptations. These shorter time periods allow for progress in one area without loss in others. However, training phases must be planned appropriately throughout the mesocycle to ensure that all priorities are addressed. For example, an 8-week mesocycle focusing primarily on strength could include a 1-week phase of endurance training and a 1- or 2-week phase of hypertrophy work in order to maintain the conditioning goals and body composition the person may also desire. The following are different types of training phases that could be included in a mesocycle to address different priorities.

- *Transitional phase.* This phase is typically the first week of a mesocycle and is characterized by low-intensity and low-volume training. This phase is commonly used to begin a mesocycle when the previous mesocycle ended with high-intensity strength or power phases. During this week, assessments are done to measure progress and to identify any adaptations achieved in the previous mesocycle. The new program is designed and introduced to the body with an emphasis on training technique. New movement patterns are learned, and the planned exercise sequence is practiced. Diet and nutritional strategies are also reviewed. The recommended volume for this phase is 1 or 2 sets per exercise for about 10 to 12 repetitions.

- *Endurance phase.* These phases typically consist of lower intensity and higher volume routines. Muscular and cardiovascular endurance is the primary focus. However, this is also a logical phase for focusing on repetitive performance of new or difficult exercises because the intensity loads are low, which will help with attempting to master new movement patterns. Exercises that require different stabilization strategies or have high balance demands are ideal for additional practice during these phases. Further descriptive titles can be used for a phase if endurance weeks are combined with other complementary phases, such as a *transitional-endurance phase* or an *endurance-hypertrophy phase.* Volume recommendations range from 1 to 3 sets for about 15 to 20 reps per exercise but occasionally are prescribed with as high as 50 reps in extreme cases.

- *Hypertrophy phase.* These phases are designed to apply the greatest combinations of intensity and volume in order to elicit muscle hypertrophy or muscle growth. This overlap of increased intensity and the maintenance of high to moderate volume also makes these phases highly metabolic and induces greater hormonal responses than other training phases, making them great for body-fat reduction as well as hypertrophy. Hypertrophy phases can be appropriate even for those people not interested in large increases of muscle mass, as long as exercise selection and volume for specific muscles are properly planned. Recommendations for sets and repetitions span from 3 to 5 sets per exercise for 8 to 12 repetitions. Hypertrophy training covers a wide range of time under tension, so more descriptive titles can be used to designate the training priorities, such as *hypertrophy-endurance phases* or *hypertrophy-strength phases.*

- *Strength phase.* These phases are characterized by high levels of intensity and reduced volumes of work. Greater rest periods and slower training tempos are also typically implemented to maximize motor unit recruitment. These phases focus on more neural and intramuscular adaptations than hypertrophy and endurance phases. Stability is a prerequisite for maximal strength; therefore, fewer exercises are selected and fewer positioning options and techniques are used that require high balance demands. Different titles may be used for strength phases that overlap with other training phases, such as *strength-hypertrophy phases* and *strength-power phases.* Volume recommendations are from 5 to 8 sets with 3 to 5 repetitions per exercise. With these recommendations, you can see why most people prefer combinations of hypertrophy and strength because this many sets of heavy loads are often too high risk for perceived benefits.

- *Power phase.* To produce power, the speed or rate of force production is as important, if not more so, as the amount of force produced. For this reason, power phases of training are characterized by the use of moderate-intensity and even low-intensity loads, with low volumes of sets and repetitions and faster tempos. Power training is difficult with standard resistance exercise movements because a proportional amount of effort that does not promote gains in power must be spent on decelerating the weight loads. Power training will often incorporate different more ballistic movements such as cleans, snatches, plyometric exercises, and medicine ball throws. Power training exacts a high neural demand for the quick productions and reductions of force, plus the increased need for dynamic stability and balance. Therefore, volume recommendations for power typically range from 3 to 5 sets of 5 to 10 reps.

The division of a macrocycle into manageable mesocycles and the division of mesocycles into the various training phases may seem like a difficult process, but it is well worth the effort. Basically, this can be done by clearly identifying the goals that a person would like to achieve for an upcoming year, which sets the priorities for the macrocycle. Whether the overall goals are related to endurance, strength, hypertrophy, or weight loss, the next step is to create subgoals that are set at reasonable time periods throughout the year and then design the appropriate mesocycles to help achieve them. Then remember to include a few phases of other types of training in each mesocycle to be sure there is a somewhat balanced approach to meeting the overall goals. Figure 9.1 provides an example of an actual macrocycle that was created recently for a middle-aged healthy executive who is serious about fitness. This person's overall goals include improved conditioning, increased muscularity, enhanced strength and stability, and superior performance in a few recreational athletic activities that the person enjoys. Sound like anyone you know?

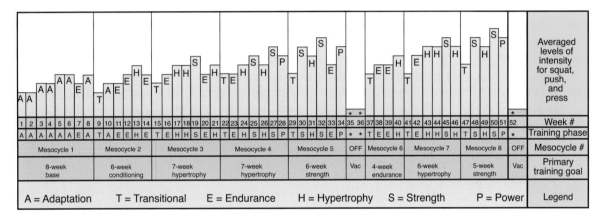

Figure 9.1 Sample macrocycle for balanced fitness.

Sample Routines

To provide a routine for any individual, I must first perform an extremely comprehensive assessment in order to identify the person's training needs. This process includes a postural assessment, general movement pattern assessment, gait assessment, and an isolated joint mobility and stability analysis designed to determine joint integrity and identify muscular imbalances. Similar assessments may be available to you and are highly recommended. Without such an assessment, it is difficult to establish needs and set performance goals. Your program would probably lack the specific movements or even the required general movement patterns needed to make sustained progress.

Therefore, the following sample routines are unlikely to address all your specific needs or to optimally accomplish your individual goals. Instead, they are presented as mere samples of how a resistance training routine could be organized in a balanced manner. The problem is that very few people presently have a balanced body. As a result, they would actually need an imbalanced program in order to restore posture, strengthen weak links, and correct muscular imbalances. However, these routines, if practiced with the proper technique and within the appropriate intensity and volume, should provide for challenging, safe, and pain-free exercise barring any present injuries. Try them, learn from them, and then try to organize your own routines based on your overall program design. It is also strongly advised that you consult with a qualified professional to help with your program design as well as your assessment.

Volume for any routine should be purposely manipulated during each phase of a mesocycle. The sets, repetitions, and tempos recommended in the following sample routines demonstrate how changes in volume are correlated with changes in intensity as they relate to the specific weekly phases. However, since the routines are presented merely as examples, so are the volume recommendations. Consider these simply as guidelines for you to consider when designing your own resistance training programs.

Base Fitness Routine

Tables 9.3 and 9.4 depict what may be an initial whole-body routine that attempts to address frequent needs and common goals of individuals who have not been recently training on a regular basis. It is referred to as a "base routine" because when a person first begins resistance training after a layoff or for the first time, the priority is to establish a fitness "base" or foundation on which all other future routines and programs will be built. Core activation exercises are immediately introduced to help with integration of the suggested breathing methods and to provide for better control of intra-abdominal and intra-thoracic pressure for improved trunk stabilization.

The trunk, lower body, and upper body exercises selected promote the development of general movement patterns and also target the various subsystems responsible for helping develop better pelvic-spinal stability. Development of good posture and increased spinal control with particular focus on improving lumbar flexion and thoracic extension are also priorities of a base routine. No rotational movements of the spine are yet prescribed because these movements may induce high amounts of compensation in an immobile and unstable spine. The set, repetition, and tempo recommendations are consistent with general strength, conditioning, and stability development, with a chance of providing moderate hypertrophy for those who are at this stage.

Full-Body Routine

The sample routine in tables 9.5 and 9.6 may be more appropriate for the individual who is presently on a regular exercise schedule. For this routine, it is assumed that the person has good development of core control, pelvic-spinal stability, and proficiency in performance of all general movement patterns. Therefore, more attention can be directed to aesthetic-based goals because structural needs have been addressed and a solid fitness base has been established. More challenging compound movements have been added as well as a few isolated movements for certain muscle groups to help improve aesthetics and performance. There may need to be a few mesocycles in between the first sample routine (base routine) and this more advanced whole-body routine. The differences may not be too apparent at first glance but can be quickly realized once you have experienced them.

Advanced Split Routine

If a person is ready to increase training frequency and wants greater amounts of muscle strengthening, hypertrophy, or conditioning, then split routines are the next step. Split routines divide the body into two or more sections in order to be able to train more frequently, increase total volume, and still allow for adequate recovery. These routines emphasize training only certain areas of the body while avoiding others. There are many methods for dividing muscle groups into split routines depending on the weekly frequency of training sessions. The example shown in tables 9.7 through 9.10 is a four-day split that uses a push-pull emphasis for designing and splitting the routines. Biceps are switched to push days while triceps are substituted on the pull days in order to provide better arm recovery for pushing and pulling. I call these routines anterior and posterior splits because each routine will emphasize either muscle groups on the front of the body or on the back. True push-pull routines and upper-lower routines are also very common examples of

TABLE 9.3 Base Strength Development A

7-week mesocycle	Week 1	Week 2	Week 3	Week 4	Week 5	Week 6	Week 7	Notes
PHASE	TRANSITIONAL	ENDURANCE	HYPERTROPHY-ENDURANCE	HYPERTROPHY-STRENGTH	ENDURANCE	HYPERTROPHY	HYPERTROPHY-STRENGTH	
Tempo	3121	3121	3121	3121	3121	3121	3121	
Volume: Sets × reps	2 × 10-12	2 × 17-20	1-3 × 12-15	1-4 × 8-10	2 × 17-20	1-3 × 10-12	1-4 × 8-10	
Warm-up	Recumbent bike 10 min Active stretching, Four-Point Core Activation							
FIRST CIRCUIT								
Dumbbell Reverse Lunge	2 × 10-12	2 × 17-20	1 × 12-15	1 × 8-10	2 × 17-20	1 × 10-12	1 × 8-10	Unilateral
Cable One-Arm Decline Chest Press	2 × 10-12	2 × 17-20	1 × 12-15	1 × 8-10	2 × 17-20	1 × 10-12	1 × 8-10	Lunge position
Cable Ham Flexion	2 × 10-12	2 × 17-20	1 × 12-15	1 × 8-10	2 × 17-20	1 × 10-12	1 × 8-10	Unilateral
Cable One-Arm Low Lat Row	2 × 10-12	2 × 17-20	1 × 12-15	1 × 8-10	2 × 17-20	1 × 10-12	1 × 8-10	Lunge position
Bench Single Bent-Leg Hip Flexion	2 × 10-12	2 × 17-20	1 × 12-15	1 × 8-10	2 × 17-20	1 × 10-12	1 × 8-10	+ incline = + intensity
SECOND CIRCUIT								
Barbell Squat	2 × 10-12	2 × 17-20	3 × 12-15	3 × 8-10	2 × 17-20	3 × 10-12	3 × 8-10	Shoulder-width stance
Dumbbell Median Plane Shoulder Press	2 × 10-12	2 × 17-20	3 × 12-15	3 × 8-10	2 × 17-20	3 × 10-12	3 × 8-10	With bench inclined to 45-60 degrees
Cable One-Arm Lat Pull-Up	2 × 10-12	2 × 17-20	3 × 12-15	3 × 8-10	2 × 17-20	3 × 10-12	3 × 8-10	Focus on scapular downward rotation
Cable Hip Abduction	2 × 10-12	2 × 17-20	3 × 12-15	3 × 8-10	2 × 17-20	3 × 10-12	3 × 8-10	Alternate each set
Flat Bench Reverse Trunk Flexion	2 × 10-12	2 × 17-20	3 × 12-15	3 × 8-10	2 × 17-20	3 × 10-12	3 × 8-10	+ incline = + intensity
SUPPLEMENTAL								
Cable Shoulder External Rotation	1-2 × 10-12	1-2 × 10-12	1-2 × 10-12	1-2 × 10-12	1-2 × 10-12	1-2 × 10-12	1-2 × 10-12	15 degrees of shoulder abduction

TABLE 9.4   Base Strength Development B

7-week mesocycle	Week 1	Week 2	Week 3	Week 4	Week 5	Week 6	Week 7	Notes
PHASE	TRANSITIONAL	ENDURANCE	HYPERTROPHY-ENDURANCE	HYPERTROPHY-STRENGTH	ENDURANCE	HYPERTROPHY	HYPERTROPHY-STRENGTH	
Tempo	3121	3121	3121	3121	3121	3121	3121	
Volume: Sets × reps	2 × 10-12	2 × 17-20	1-3 × 12-15	1-3 × 8-10	2 × 17-20	1-3 × 10-12	1-4 × 8-10	
Warm-up	Recumbent bike 10 min Active stretching, Quadraplex							
FIRST CIRCUIT								
Dumbbell Side Lunge	2 × 10-12	2 × 17-20	1 × 12-15	1 × 8-10	2 × 17-20	1 × 10-12	1 × 8-10	Unilateral
Dumbbell One-Arm and One-Leg Frontal Plane Shoulder Press	2 × 10-12	2 × 17-20	1 × 12-15	1 × 8-10	2 × 17-20	1 × 10-12	1 × 8-10	Move to a seated position with heavy weight, maintain unilateral arm movement
Cable One-Arm Lat Pull-Down	2 × 10-12	2 × 17-20	1 × 12-15	1 × 8-10	2 × 17-20	1 × 10-12	1 × 8-10	Lunge position
Cable Quad Extension	2 × 10-12	2 × 17-20	1 × 12-15	1 × 8-10	2 × 17-20	1 × 10-12	1 × 8-10	Unilateral
Cable One-Arm Shoulder Row	2 × 10-12	2 × 17-20	1 × 12-15	1 × 8-10	2 × 17-20	1 × 10-12	1 × 8-10	Lunge position
SECOND CIRCUIT								
Dumbbell Deadlift	2 × 10-12	2 × 17-20	3 × 12-15	3 × 8-10	2 × 17-20	3 × 10-12	4 × 8-10	Wide stance
Dumbbell and Bench Chest Press	2 × 10-12	2 × 17-20	3 × 12-15	3 × 8-10	2 × 17-20	3 × 10-12	4 × 8-10	Try on Swiss ball weeks 2 and 5
Cable Overhead Lat Extension	2 × 10-12	2 × 17-20	3 × 12-15	3 × 8-10	2 × 17-20	3 × 10-12	4 × 8-10	Standing
Machine Ham Flexion	2 × 10-12	2 × 17-20	3 × 12-15	3 × 8-10	2 × 17-20	3 × 10-12	4 × 8-10	Bilateral
Flat Bench Reverse Trunk Flexion	2 × 10-12	2 × 17-20	3 × 12-15	3 × 8-10	2 × 17-20	3 × 10-12	4 × 8-10	+ incline = + intensity
SUPPLEMENTAL								
Machine Calf Extension	1-2 × 15-17	1-2 × 15-17	1-2 × 15-17	1-2 × 15-17	1-2 × 15-17	1-2 × 15-17	1-2 × 15-17	
Machine Tib Flexion	1 × 15-17	1 × 15-17	1 × 15-17	1 × 15-17	1 × 15-17	1 × 15-17	1 × 15-17	Each leg

TABLE 9.5 Full-Body Fitness A

7-week mesocycle	Week 1	Week 2	Week 3	Week 4	Week 5	Week 6	Week 7	Notes
PHASE	TRANSITIONAL	ENDURANCE	HYPERTROPHY-ENDURANCE	HYPERTROPHY-STRENGTH	ENDURANCE	HYPERTROPHY	HYPERTROPHY-STRENGTH	
Tempo	3121	2121	3121	4122	2121	3121	4122	
Volume: Sets × reps	2 × 10-12	2 × 17-20	2-3 × 12-15	1-4 × 8-10	2 × 17-20	2-3 × 10-12	1-4 × 8-10	
Warm-up	Recumbent bike 10 min. Active stretching, Four-Point Core Activation, Quadraplex							
FIRST CIRCUIT								
Dumbbell Side Lunge	2 × 10-12	2 × 17-20	2 × 12-15	1 × 8-10	2 × 17-20	2 × 10-12	1 × 8-10	Unilateral
Cable One-Arm Decline Chest Press	2 × 10-12	2 × 17-20	2 × 12-15	1 × 8-10	2 × 17-20	2 × 10-12	1 × 8-10	Lunge position
Cable Ham Flexion	2 × 10-12	2 × 17-20	2 × 12-15	1 × 8-10	2 × 17-20	2 × 10-12	1 × 8-10	Unilateral
Cable One-Arm Low Lat Row	2 × 10-12	2 × 17-20	2 × 12-15	1 × 8-10	2 × 17-20	2 × 10-12	1 × 8-10	Lunge position
Cable Trunk Rotation With Flexion	2 × 10-12	2 × 17-20	2 × 12-15	1 × 8-10	2 × 17-20	2 × 10-12	1 × 8-10	Lunge position
SECOND CIRCUIT								
Barbell Squat	2 × 10-12	2 × 17-20	3 × 12-15	4 × 8-10	2 × 17-20	3 × 10-12	4 × 8-10	Shoulder-width stance
Dumbbell Incline Press	2 × 10-12	2 × 17-20	3 × 12-15	4 × 8-10	2 × 17-20	3 × 10-12	4 × 8-10	Median plane; see page 151, with bench inclined to 30-45 degrees
Machine Seated Leg Press	2 × 10-12	2 × 17-20	3 × 12-15	4 × 8-10	2 × 17-20	3 × 10-12	4 × 8-10	Superset wide-narrow
Machine Lat Pull-Up	2 × 10-12	2 × 17-20	3 × 12-15	4 × 8-10	2 × 17-20	3 × 10-12	4 × 8-10	Emphasis on scapular movement
Cable One-Arm 90-Degree Triceps Extension	2 × 10-12	2 × 17-20	3 × 12-15	4 × 8-10	2 × 17-20	3 × 10-12	4 × 8-10	Lunge position, bilateral
Machine Calf Extension/Tib Flexion	2 × 10-12	2 × 17-20	3 × 12-15	4 × 8-10	2 × 17-20	3 × 10-12	4 × 8-10	Substitute 1 set Machine Tib Flexion
SUPPLEMENTAL								
Cable Shoulder External Rotation	1-2 × 10-12	1-2 × 10-12	1-2 × 10-12	1-2 × 10-12	1-2 × 10-12	1-2 × 10-12	1-2 × 10-12	15 degrees of shoulder abduction

TABLE 9.6 Full-Body Fitness B

7-week mesocycle	Week 1	Week 2	Week 3	Week 4	Week 5	Week 6	Week 7	Notes
PHASE	TRANSITIONAL	ENDURANCE	HYPERTROPHY-ENDURANCE	HYPERTROPHY-STRENGTH	ENDURANCE	HYPERTROPHY	HYPERTROPHY-STRENGTH	
Tempo	3121	2121	3121	4122	2121	3121	4122	
Volume: Sets × reps	2 × 10-12	2 × 17-20	2-3 × 12-15	1-4 × 8-10	2 × 17-20	2-3 × 10-12	1-4 × 8-10	
Warm-up	Recumbent bike 10 min / Active stretching, Four-Point Core Activation, Quadraplex							
FIRST CIRCUIT								
Med Ball Traveling Lunge	2 × 10-12	2 × 17-20	2 × 12-15	1 × 8-10	2 × 17-20	2 × 10-12	1 × 8-10	Alternate legs
Dumbbell and Swiss Ball One-Arm Incline Chest Press	2 × 10-12	2 × 17-20	2 × 12-15	1 × 8-10	2 × 17-20	2 × 10-12	1 × 8-10	Stabilize trunk and neck
Dumbbell Deadlift	2 × 10-12	2 × 17-20	2 × 12-15	1 × 8-10	2 × 17-20	2 × 10-12	1 × 8-10	Wide stance
Cable One-Arm Lat Pull-Down	2 × 10-12	2 × 17-20	2 × 12-15	1 × 8-10	2 × 17-20	2 × 10-12	1 × 8-10	Lunge position
Cable Hip Abduction	2 × 10-12	2 × 17-20	2 × 12-15	1 × 8-10	2 × 17-20	2 × 10-12	1 × 8-10	Focus on pelvic stabilization
SECOND CIRCUIT								
Dumbbell Reverse Lunge	2 × 10-12	2 × 17-20	3 × 12-15	4 × 8-10	2 × 17-20	3 × 10-12	4 × 8-10	Alternate
Barbell and Bench Chest Press	2 × 10-12	2 × 17-20	3 × 12-15	4 × 8-10	2 × 17-20	3 × 10-12	4 × 8-10	Keep proper range of motion
Machine Ham Flexion	2 × 10-12	2 × 17-20	3 × 12-15	4 × 8-10	2 × 17-20	3 × 10-12	4 × 8-10	Bilateral
Cable Seated Low Lat Row	2 × 10-12	2 × 17-20	3 × 12-15	4 × 8-10	2 × 17-20	3 × 10-12	4 × 8-10	Focus on posture
Machine Calf Extension	2 × 10-12	2 × 17-20	3 × 12-15	4 × 8-10	2 × 17-20	3 × 10-12	4 × 8-10	Keep reps at the higher range
Dumbbell Shoulder Row	2 × 10-12	2 × 17-20	3 × 12-15	4 × 8-10	2 × 17-20	3 × 10-12	4 × 8-10	Switch to high cable when heavy
Swiss Ball Reverse Trunk Flexion	2 × 10-12	2 × 17-20	3 × 12-15	4 × 8-10	2 × 17-20	3 × 10-12	4 × 8-10	Focus on lumbar flexion

TABLE 9.7 Anterior Split A

7-week mesocycle	Week 1	Week 2	Week 3	Week 4	Week 5	Week 6	Week 7	Notes
PHASE	TRANSITIONAL	ENDURANCE	HYPERTROPHY-ENDURANCE	HYPERTROPHY-STRENGTH	ENDURANCE	HYPERTROPHY	STRENGTH	
Tempo	3121	2121	3121	4122	2121	3121	4122	
Volume: Sets × reps	2 × 10-12	2 × 17-20	2-3 × 12-15	1-4 × 8-10	2 × 17-20	2-3 × 10-12	1-4 × 6-10	
Warm-up	Recumbent bike 10 min Active stretching, Quadraplex, Bent-Leg Raises							
FIRST CIRCUIT								
Dumbbell Side Lunge	2 × 10-12	2 × 17-20	2 × 12-15	2 × 8-10	2 × 17-20	2 × 10-12	2 × 8-10	Unilateral
Cable One-Arm Decline Chest Press	2 × 10-12	2 × 17-20	2 × 12-15	2 × 8-10	2 × 17-20	2 × 10-12	2 × 8-10	Lunge position
Cable Quad Extension	2 × 10-12	2 × 17-20	2 × 12-15	2 × 8-10	2 × 17-20	2 × 10-12	2 × 8-10	Flex hip each rep
Cable One-Arm 90-Degree Biceps Flexion	2 × 10-12	2 × 17-20	2 × 12-15	2 × 8-10	2 × 17-20	2 × 10-12	2 × 8-10	Lunge position, unilateral
Cable Trunk Rotation With Flexion	2 × 10-12	2 × 17-20	2 × 12-15	2 × 8-10	2 × 17-20	2 × 10-12	2 × 8-10	Lunge position
SECOND CIRCUIT								
Med Ball Traveling Lunge	2 × 10-12	2 × 17-20	3 × 12-15	Skip	2 × 17-20	3 × 10-12	Skip	Alternate steps
Dumbbell and Bench Chest Press	2 × 10-12	2 × 17-20	3 × 12-15	4 × 8-10	2 × 17-20	3 × 10-12	4 × 6-8	Maintain spinal and scapular positioning
Machine Seated Leg Press (high reps)	2 × 15	1 × 35, 1 × 25	1 × 25, 2 × 20	1 × 20, 3 × 15	1 × 35, 1 × 25	1 × 25, 2 × 20	1 × 20, 3 × 15	Follow rep scheme
Dumbbell Median Plane Shoulder Press	2 × 10-12	2 × 17-20	3 × 12-15	4 × 8-10	2 × 17-20	3 × 10-12	4 × 6-8	Incline bench to 45-60 degrees
Dumbbell Biceps Flexion With Supination	2 × 10-12	2 × 17-20	3 × 12-15	4 × 8-10	2 × 17-20	3 × 10-12	4 × 6-8	Offset dumbbells for targeting supination
Swiss Ball Reverse Trunk Flexion	2 × 10-12	2 × 17-20	3 × 12-15	4 × 8-10	2 × 17-20	3 × 10-12	4 × 6-8	Focus on lumbar flexion
SUPPLEMENTAL								
Machine Tib Flexion	1-2 × 12-15	1-2 × 12-15	1-2 × 12-15	1-2 × 12-15	1-2 × 12-15	1-2 × 12-15	1-2 × 12-15	

TABLE 9.8 Posterior Split A

7-week mesocycle	Week 1	Week 2	Week 3	Week 4	Week 5	Week 6	Week 7	Notes
PHASE	TRANSITIONAL	ENDURANCE	HYPERTROPHY-ENDURANCE	HYPERTROPHY-STRENGTH	ENDURANCE	HYPERTROPHY	STRENGTH	
Tempo	3121	2121	3121	4122	2121	3121	4122	
Volume: Sets × reps	2 × 10-12	2 × 17-20	2-3 × 12-15	1-4 × 8-10	2 × 17-20	2-3 × 10-12	1-4 × 8-10	
Warm-up	Recumbent bike 10 min Active stretching, Four-Point Core Activation, Quadraplex							
FIRST CIRCUIT								
Cable Ham Flexion	2 × 10-12	2 × 17-20	2 × 12-15	2 × 8-10	2 × 17-20	2 × 10-12	2 × 8-10	Extend hip each rep
Cable One-Arm Low Lat Row	2 × 10-12	2 × 17-20	2 × 12-15	2 × 8-10	2 × 17-20	2 × 10-12	2 × 8-10	Lunge position
Cable Hip Abduction	2 × 10-12	2 × 17-20	2 × 12-15	2 × 8-10	2 × 17-20	2 × 10-12	2 × 8-10	Pelvic stabilization
Cable One-Arm Shoulder Row	2 × 10-12	2 × 17-20	2 × 12-15	2 × 8-10	2 × 17-20	2 × 10-12	2 × 8-10	Lunge position
Cable One-Arm 90-Degree Triceps Extension	2 × 10-12	2 × 17-20	2 × 12-15	2 × 8-10	2 × 17-20	2 × 10-12	2 × 8-10	Lunge position
SECOND CIRCUIT								
45-Degree Hip Extension	2 × 10-12	2 × 17-20	3 × 12-15	4 × 8-10	2 × 17-20	3 × 10-12	4 × 8-10	Maintain optimal posture throughout movement
Machine Lat Pull-Up	2 × 10-12	2 × 17-20	3 × 12-15	4 × 8-10	2 × 17-20	3 × 10-12	4 × 8-10	Emphasis on scapular movement
Machine Ham Flexion	2 × 10-12	2 × 17-20	3 × 12-15	4 × 8-10	2 × 17-20	3 × 10-12	4 × 8-10	Bilateral
Dumbbell Shoulder Row	2 × 10-12	2 × 17-20	3 × 12-15	4 × 8-10	2 × 17-20	3 × 10-12	4 × 8-10	Switch to high cable when heavy
Cable Zero-Degree Triceps Extension	2 × 10-12	2 × 17-20	3 × 12-15	4 × 8-10	2 × 17-20	3 × 10-12	4 × 8-10	Emphasis on scapular positioning
Machine Calf Extension	2 × 10-12	2 × 17-20	3 × 12-15	4 × 10-12	2 × 17-20	3 × 12-15	4 × 10-12	Keep reps at the higher range
SUPPLEMENTAL								
Cable Shoulder External Rotation	1-2 × 10-12	1-2 × 10-12	1-2 × 10-12	1-2 × 10-12	1-2 × 10-12	1-2 × 10-12	1-2 × 10-12	15 degrees of shoulder abduction

Table 9.9 Anterior Split B

7-week mesocycle	Week 1	Week 2	Week 3	Week 4	Week 5	Week 6	Week 7	Notes
PHASE	TRANSITIONAL	ENDURANCE	HYPERTROPHY-ENDURANCE	HYPERTROPHY-STRENGTH	ENDURANCE	HYPERTROPHY	STRENGTH	
Tempo	3121	2121	3121	4122	2121	3121	4122	
Volume: Sets × reps	2 × 10-12	2 × 17-20	2-3 × 12-15	1-4 × 8-10	2 × 17-20	2-3 × 10-12	1-4 × 6-10	
Warm-up	Recumbent bike 10 min Active stretching, Quadraplex, Bent-Leg Raises							
FIRST CIRCUIT								
Dumbbell Reverse Lunge	2 × 10-12	2 × 17-20	2 × 12-15	2 × 8-10	2 × 17-20	2 × 10-12	2 × 8-10	Bilateral
Dumbbell One-Arm and One-Leg Frontal Plane Shoulder Press	2 × 10-12	2 × 17-20	2 × 12-15	2 × 8-10	2 × 17-20	2 × 10-12	2 × 8-10	Move to a seated position with heavy weight, maintain unilateral arm movement
Dumbbell One-Arm Snatch	2 × 10-12	2 × 10-12	2 × 10-12	2 × 10-12	2 × 10-12	2 × 10-12	2 × 10-12	Focus on technique
Swiss Ball Double-Leg Hip Flexion	2 × 10-12	2 × 17-20	2 × 12-15	2 × 8-10	2 × 17-20	2 × 10-12	2 × 8-10	Single- or double-leg depending on ability
Swiss Ball Trunk Flexion	2 × 10-12	2 × 17-20	2 × 12-15	2 × 8-10	2 × 17-20	2 × 10-12	2 × 8-10	Stabilize head-neck position
SECOND CIRCUIT								
Barbell Squat (high reps)	2 × 20	1 × 35, 1 × 25	1 × 25, 2 × 20	1 × 20, 3 × 15	1 × 35, 1 × 25	1 × 20, 2 × 15	1 × 15, 3 × 10	Follow repetition scheme
Flat Bench Reverse Trunk Flexion	2 × 10-12	2 × 17-20	3 × 12-15	4 × 8-10	2 × 17-20	3 × 10-12	4 × 6-8	Incline bench as needed for repetition scheme
Dumbbell Incline Chest Press	2 × 10-12	2 × 17-20	3 × 12-15	4 × 8-10	2 × 17-20	3 × 10-12	4 × 6-8	45-degree, horizontal plane; see page 151 for technique (but adjust bench to 30 to 45 degrees)
Machine Quad Extension	2 × 12-15	2 × 12-15	2 × 12-15	Skip	2 × 12-15	2 × 12-15	Skip	Keep weight low to moderate
Machine Trunk Rotation	2 × 10-12	2 × 17-20	3 × 12-15	4 × 8-10	2 × 17-20	3 × 10-12	4 × 6-8	Limit exercise ROM to active ROM
Dumbbell Biceps Flexion With Supination	2 × 10-12	2 × 17-20	3 × 12-15	4 × 8-10	2 × 17-20	3 × 10-12	4 × 6-8	Offset dumbbells for targeting supination
SUPPLEMENTAL								
Squat Rack Push-Up	1-2 sets to failure	1-2 sets to failure	1-2 sets to failure	1-2 sets to failure	1-2 sets to failure	1-2 sets to failure	1-2 sets to failure	

TABLE 9.10 **Posterior Split B**

7-week mesocycle	Week 1	Week 2	Week 3	Week 4	Week 5	Week 6	Week 7	Notes
PHASE	TRANSITIONAL	ENDURANCE	HYPERTROPHY-ENDURANCE	HYPERTROPHY-STRENGTH	ENDURANCE	HYPERTROPHY	STRENGTH	
Tempo	3121	2121	3121	4122	2121	3121	4122	
Volume: Sets × reps	2 × 10-12	2 × 17-20	2-3 × 12-15	1-4 × 8-10	2 × 17-20	2-3 × 10-12	1-4 × 8-10	
Warm-up	Recumbent bike 10 min Active stretching, Four-Point Core Activation, Quadraplex							
FIRST CIRCUIT								
Dumbbell One-Leg Hip Extension	2 × 10-12	2 × 17-20	2 × 12-15	Skip	2 × 17-20	2 × 10-12	Skip	Focus on technique
Cable One-Arm Lat Pull-Down	2 × 10-12	2 × 17-20	2 × 12-15	2 × 8-10	2 × 17-20	2 × 10-12	2 × 8-10	Lunge position
Machine Ham Flexion	2 × 10-12	2 × 17-20	2 × 12-15	2 × 8-10	2 × 17-20	2 × 10-12	2 × 8-10	Stabilize pelvis
Cable One-Arm Shoulder Row	2 × 10-12	2 × 17-20	2 × 12-15	2 × 8-10	2 × 17-20	2 × 10-12	2 × 8-10	Lunge position
Cable Zero-Degree Triceps Extension	2 × 10-12	2 × 17-20	2 × 12-15	2 × 8-10	2 × 17-20	2 × 10-12	2 × 8-10	Standing
SECOND CIRCUIT								
Barbell Hip Extension	2 × 10-12	2 × 17-20	3 × 12-15	4 × 8-10	2 × 17-20	3 × 10-12	4 × 8-10	Focus on technique
Cable Seated Low Lat Row	2 × 10-12	2 × 17-20	3 × 12-15	4 × 8-10	2 × 17-20	3 × 10-12	4 × 8-10	Emphasis on scapular-thoracic movement
Cable One-Arm 90-Degree Triceps Extension	2 × 10-12	2 × 17-20	3 × 12-15	4 × 8-10	2 × 17-20	3 × 10-12	4 × 8-10	Lunge position
Machine Lat Pull-Up	2 × 10-12	2 × 17-20	3 × 12-15	4 × 8-10	2 × 17-20	3 × 10-12	4 × 8-10	Emphasis on scapular movement
Squat Rack Push-Up	2 × 10-12	2 × 17-20	3 × 12-15	4 × 8-10	2 × 17-20	3 × 10-12	4 × 8-10	Median plane
Machine Calf Extension	2 × 25	2 × 20	3 × 15	3 × 15	2 × 20	3 × 15	3 × 15	Keep reps at higher range
SUPPLEMENTAL								
Dumbbell Horizontal Plane External Shoulder Rotation	1-2 × 10-12	1-2 × 10-12	1-2 × 10-12	1-2 × 10-12	1-2 × 10-12	1-2 × 10-12	1-2 × 10-12	

four-day-a-week splits that could be tried on different mesocycles. Be sure to follow the listed sequence of each routine even if days are missed, because a person could easily begin training the body in an unbalanced manner if performing more of one split than another.

Programming and Periodization Tips

When beginning to implement periodization, remember that a good base must be preestablished with structural and health needs already addressed. In the initial phases of training, a person can typically make progress through the use of predetermined and consistent amounts of sets and repetitions while linearly progressing the intensity. This means simply that the resistance load is increased whenever repetition goals for a given set become easy to accomplish. However, linear progression is most often short lived, and plateaus will eventually occur that will hinder progress or even reverse it.

When you need to begin using periodization, simply start one step at a time. Exercise programming and periodization models are not mastered over night. Too much variation and random changes can supply an overload of information and apply too much varied stress for the neuromuscular system to adapt to. This can be as inefficient as no variation at all. Consider these tips on periodization:

1. Break macrocycles up into manageable smaller programs or mesocycles.

2. Design each mesocycle with a certain number of the various endurance, hypertrophy, strength, and power phases depending on specific training goals.

3. Begin each mesocycle with a transitional phase.

4. Practice movements and integrate positioning options that require more stabilization and greater balance demands while intensity is low.

5. Use more stabilized positioning during phases in which increased motor unit recruitment and maximal strength are desired.

6. Keep a reciprocal relationship between intensity and overall volume.

7. When decreasing repetitions, increase sets, increase rest periods, and select fewer movements for each muscle group.

8. Make small adjustments to sequence according to the priorities of the training phase.

9. Never compromise structural integrity and overall health needs for the pursuit of specific training goals.

10. Always integrate and adhere to all elements of proper exercise technique. What *is* done can only be as efficient as *how* it is done.

I hope this book proves to be a valuable resource for assisting you in the pursuit of improved health, enhanced performance, and a higher level of personal fitness. By learning and following the training principles and exercise techniques presented in this book, you should be able to begin pursuing all of your fitness goals in a safe and efficient manner. It is my hope that you will also be empowered to select those professionals who will assist you and guide you along your path toward optimal fitness. Remember that it is great to train hard, but even better to train smart.

Bibliography

Aaberg, E. 2000. *Resistance training instruction.* Champaign, IL: Human Kinetics.

Aaberg, E. 2001. *Resistance training instruction video series: The trunk.* Champaign, IL: Human Kinetics.

Aaberg, E. 2001. *Resistance training instruction video series: The lower body.* Champaign, IL: Human Kinetics.

Aaberg, E. 2001. *Resistance training instruction video series: The upper body.* Champaign, IL: Human Kinetics.

Alter, M. 1996. *Science of flexibility.* 2nd ed. Champaign, IL: Human Kinetics.

National Strength and Conditioning Association. 1994. *Essentials of strength and conditioning,* ed. by T. Baechle and R. Earle. Champaign, IL: Human Kinetics.

Bompa, T., and L. Cornacchia. 1998. *Serious strength training.* Champaign, IL: Human Kinetics.

Brown, L., and V. Ferrigno. 2005. *Training for speed, agility, and quickness.* 2nd ed. Champaign, IL: Human Kinetics.

Calais-Germain, B. 1993. *Anatomy of movement.* Seattle, WA: Eastland Press.

Check, P. 1995. *Program design.* Encinitas, CA: C.H.E.C.K. Institute.

Check, P. 1995. *Scientific back training.* Encinitas, CA: C.H.E.C.K. Institute.

Check, P. 1996. *Dynamic medicine ball training.* Video and correspondence course. Encinitas, CA: C.H.E.C.K. Institute.

Check, P. 1998. *Golf conditioning.* Encinitas, CA: C.H.E.C.K. Institute.

Check, P. 1998. *Scientific core training.* Video and correspondence course. Encinitas, CA: C.H.E.C.K. Institute.

Check, P. 1999. *The outer unit.* ptonthenet.com: Personal Training on the Net.

Check, P. 2000. *Movement that matters.* Encinitas, CA: C.H.E.C.K. Institute.

Chu, D. 1998. *Jumping into plyometrics.* 2nd ed. Champaign, IL: Leisure Press.

Clark, M. 2001. *Integrated training for the new millennium.* Thousand Oaks, CA: National Academy of Sports Medicine.

Enoka, R. 2002. *Neuromechanics of human movement.* 3rd ed. Champaign, IL: Human Kinetics.

Fleck, S., and W. Kraemer. 1996. *Periodization breakthrough.* Ronkonkoma, NY: Advanced Research Press.

Fleck, S., and W. Kraemer. 1997. *Designing resistance training programs.* 2nd ed. Champaign, IL: Human Kinetics.

Foran, B. 2001. *High performance sports conditioning.* Champaign, IL: Human Kinetics.

Heyward, V. 2002. *Advanced fitness assessment and exercise prescription.* 4th ed. Champaign, IL: Human Kinetics.

Lephart, S., and F. Fu. 2000. *Proprioception and neuromuscular control in joint stability.* Champaign, IL: Human Kinetics.

Norkin, C., and P. Levangie. 1992. *Joint structure and function: A comprehensive analysis.* Philadelphia: F.A. Davis Company.

Poliquin, C. 1997. *The Poliquin principles.* Napa, CA: Dayton Writers Group.

Poliquin, C. 1998. *Charles Poliquin's advanced strength training certification program.* Napa, CA: Dayton Publications.

Purvis, T. 1995. *Focus on fitness.* Instructor video series. Oklahoma City: Focus on Fitness Productions.

Purvis, T. 1997. *Resistance training specialist.* The Mastery Course Manual 1. Oklahoma City: Focus on Fitness Productions.

Purvis, T. 1997. *Resistance training specialist.* The Mastery Course Manual 2. Oklahoma City: Focus on Fitness Productions.

Purvis, T. 1997. *Resistance training specialist.* The Mastery Course Manual 3. Oklahoma City: Focus on Fitness Productions.

Purvis, T. 1997. *Resistance training specialist.* The Mastery Course Manual 4. Oklahoma City: Focus on Fitness Productions.

Radcliffe, J., and R. Farentinos. 1999. *High-powered plyometrics.* Champaign, IL: Human Kinetics.

Renstrom, P.A.F.H. 1993. *Sports injuries: Basic principles of prevention and care.* Oxford: Blackwell Scientific Publications.

Richardson, C., G. Jull, P. Hodges, and J. Hides. 1999. *Therapeutic exercise for spinal segmental stabilization in low back pain.* London: Churchill Livingstone.

Schmidt, R.A., and C.A. Wrisberg. 2004. *Motor learning and performance.* 3rd ed. Champaign, IL: Human Kinetics.

Siff, M. 1998. *Facts and fallacies of fitness.* 2nd ed. Johannesburg, South Africa: M. Siff.

Siff, M. 2000. *Supertraining.* 5th ed. Denver: M. Siff. Supertraining Institute.

Vleeming, A., V. Mooney, T. Dorman, C. Snijders, and R. Stoeckart. 1997. *Movement, stability and low back pain.* New York: Churchill Livingstone.

Watkins, J. 1999. *Structure and function of the musculoskeletal system.* Champaign, IL: Human Kinetics.

Index

Note: Page numbers followed by *f* or *t* indicate a figure or table will be found on that page, respectively. Specific exercises are listed under their targeted body areas.

About the Author

Everett Aaberg has been both a teacher and practitioner of resistance training for more than 15 years. He is currently the director of fitness services and co-owner of the TELOS Performance Center in Dallas, Texas. A highly sought international presenter and consultant, Aaberg provides continuing education services for several fitness organizations and health clubs around the United States. He also serves as an instructor for the Cooper Institute, where his books are used for two of their most popular courses, The Biomechanics of Resistance Training and Optimal Performance Training.

Aaberg has been a certified personal trainer through some of the most highly accredited organizations in the United States, including American Council on Exercise (ACE), American College of Sports Medicine (ACSM), and National Academy of Sports Medicine (NASM). He is also a certified strength and conditioning specialist through the National Strength and Conditioning Association (NSCA). Aaberg was recognized as an IDEA Personal Trainer of the Year and has been regularly selected by industry and trade magazines as one of the top trainers in the country.

Aaberg holds a bachelor's degree in exercise sciences and recreation management with continuing education in exercise physiology, anatomy, kinesiology, biomechanics, and nutrition. He was a collegiate academic All-American in football and has won several state and national powerlifting championships and bodybuilding titles, including Amateur Athletic Union (AAU) and National Physique Committee (NPC) Mr. Colorado titles and the Mr. Junior America title. Aaberg lives in Dallas, Texas, and trains at the TELOS Performance Center.

Fuel and fine-tune your physique!

Get an inside look at the human form in action with more than 400 full-color illustrations. Like having an X-ray for each exercise, the detailed artwork gives you a multifaceted view of strength training not seen in any other resource. This updated bestseller also contains anatomical analysis of training injuries and preventive measures to help you exercise safely.

ISBN 978-0-7360-6368-5 • 144 pages

Armed with solid scientific principles and proven training and nutrition programs, you will gain more muscle strength, mass, and definition than ever before. Follow the general programs illustrated or tailor one to your special needs through effective manipulation of the six training phases—anatomical adaptation, hypertrophy, mixed, maximum strength, muscle definition, and transition–and proper application of the individual metabolic profile.

ISBN 978-0-7360-4266-6 • 304 pages

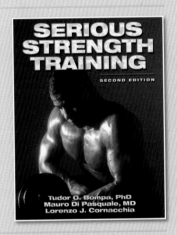

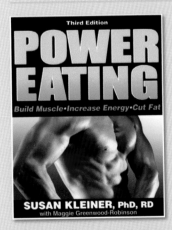

This third edition incorporates the latest nutrition principles and recommendations, specifically addressing and dispelling the myths about carbohydrate and its role in a power athlete's diet. A revised supplement rating system incorporates new IOC rules and makes the latest findings on vitamins and minerals, muscle-building products, and performance-related herbs easier to find. And the inclusion of more recipes and meal plans will provide greater variety for you on specialized eating plans.

ISBN 978-0-7360-6698-3 • 328 pages

HUMAN KINETICS
The Premier Publisher for Sports & Fitness
P.O. Box 5076, Champaign, IL 61825-5076

To place your order, U.S. customers call TOLL FREE

1-800-747-4457

In Canada call **1-800-465-7301**
In Australia call **(08) 8372 0999**
In New Zealand call **0064 9 448 1207**
In Europe call **+44 (0) 113 255 5665**

or visit **www.HumanKinetics.com**